200
SUPER SOUPS

D1258612

200

HAMLYN **ALL COLOR COOKBOOK**

SUPER SOUPS

SARA LEWIS

For my lovely father, Michael, who would eat soup
every day if he could!

An Hachette UK Company
www.hachette.co.uk

First published in Great Britain in 2009 by Hamlyn,
a division of Octopus Publishing Group Ltd,
Carmelite House, 50 Victoria Embankment,
London EC4Y 0DZ
www.octopusbooks.co.uk

This edition published in 2016

Copyright © Octopus Publishing Group Ltd 2009, 2016

Some of the recipes in this book have previously
appeared in other books published by Hamlyn

Distributed in the US by Hachette Book Group,
1290 Avenue of the Americas, 4th and 5th Floors,
New York, NY 10020

Distributed in Canada by Canadian Manda Group,
664 Annette St., Toronto, Ontario, Canada M6S 2C8

ISBN 978-0-600-63351-8

A CIP catalogue record for this book is available
from the British Library

Printed and bound in China

10 9 8 7 6 5 4 3 2 1

Standard level spoon measurement are used in all recipes.

Eggs should be medium unless otherwise stated. This book
contains dishes made with raw or lightly cooked eggs. It is
prudent for more vulnerable people such as pregnant and
nursing mothers, invalids, the elderly, babies, and young
children to avoid uncooked or lightly cooked dishes made
with eggs. Once prepared these dishes should be kept
refrigerated and used promptly.

Ovens should be preheated to the specific temperature.
If using a convection oven, follow the manufacturer's
instructions for adjusting the time and the temperature.

This book includes dishes made with nuts and nut
derivatives. It is advisable for customers with known allergic
reactions to nuts and nut derivatives and those who may
be potentially vulnerable to these allergies, such as pregnant
and nursing mothers, invalids, the elderly, babies, and
children, to avoid dishes made with nuts and nut oils.
It is also prudent to check the labels of pre-prepared
ingredients for the possible inclusion of nut derivatives.

contents

introduction

introduction

As we become ever more conscious of the benefits of eating freshly made healthy food, and the financial and environmental consequences of the huge amounts of food that we waste, there could not be a better time to return to making soups just as our mothers and grandmothers did. A homemade soup not only tastes great, but also makes a few ingredients seem like a whole lot more. They can be made at a fraction of the price of a carton of chilled soup from the supermarket and from a huge variety of ingredients. And they are surprisingly quick and easy to make. Once everything is in the saucepan they can be left to simmer while you get on with something else, requiring just 10 minutes or so at the end to finish off.

In the following pages you will find soups to appeal to all tastes, occasions, and seasons, from speedy soups that can be put together quickly after a busy day at work, to slow-cooked, hearty winter warmers, perfect for a Saturday lunch. There are elegant soups with dainty garnishes to impress dinner guests and refreshing chilled soups for the hot days of summer. The range of recipes and ingredients is vast and sometimes surprising: there are traditional meat and vegetable broths; Asian hot and sour soups; creamy smooth vegetable soups; chunky fish chowders; classics such as French onion soup; and recipes gathered from world cuisines, such as comforting chicken soup with lockshen, Indian-inspired mulligatawny, and the vibrantly colored Russian borshch.

Soups are the perfect comfort food: healthy, packed with vegetables, and, depending on the soup you choose, usually low in fat. Tucking into a bowl of steaming hot soup on a cold, dull day is like turning on the central heating from the inside and guarantees to banish the winter blues.

types of soup

Broths These chunky, clear soups are really a complete meal in a bowl and can be thickened with rice, potatoes, or legumes and mixed with lots of diced or shredded vegetables. They can be made even more substantial with the addition of tiny dumplings or pasta toward the end of cooking.

Chowders These chunky soups originated in America and contain lightly fried onions and diced potatoes simmered gently with smoked or white fish, or a mixture of flat fish and shellfish in fish stock, then finished with milk or milk and cream.

Purees Probably the most popular, these soups can be made with a huge variety of ingredients gently simmered with stock then blended in a blender or food processor at the end of cooking for a smooth, silky texture.

Bisques These rich soups are always made with fish and pureed at the end of cooking,

then generally mixed with cream or a mix of milk and cream.

Veloutés These smooth soups are thickened with a mixture of egg yolks and cream to enrich the soup at the end of the cooking time. To prevent the eggs from curdling, a ladleful of hot soup is mixed with the eggs and cream before adding to the main pot of soup. It is crucial that these soups are then heated gently and not boiled, just as you would when making a sweet custard, stirring continuously, so that the eggs thicken the soup rather than scramble.

Potages A French term used to describe unstrained soups either poured over bread or topped with a bread croute. They can also contain rice or pasta.

Consommés Ultra clear soups that are rather out of vogue now. They are made with a concentrated beef stock that is then filtered through a jelly bag with egg shells and egg white to remove any scum.

homemade stock

The best soups are those made with homemade stocks. Traditionally this was made from the bones of the Sunday roast and flavored with a few vegetable trimmings and herbs, as a way of making use of every part of a joint and using those scraps of leftover meat to make a hearty and filling meal. In today's age of recycling, it still makes excellent sense to use that scrappy-looking chicken carcass as the base for a delicious lunch or supper. And don't chuck out those refrigerator and vegetable-basket oddments, either: that slightly wrinkled carrot; those last few slightly bendy celery sticks; the stalks from that bunch of parsley or cilantro can all be put into the stock. Add the odd bay leaf from the garden or the green leek or scallion tops that are rather strong tasting and a sprinkling of peppercorns for extra flavor. The more you add the better it will be.

The secret is to add all the ingredients and then to bring the stock just to a boil, reduce the heat to a very gentle simmer so that the water barely shudders, then cook with the lid half on, half off the pan for 2 hours, or longer if you have the time. Keep the heat very low, as if it is too high you will produce a thick, muddy-looking stock.

At the end of the cooking time, taste the stock. If it seems a little thin, remove the lid and simmer for another hour or two to reduce the liquid and concentrate the flavors. Strain and allow to cool. Skim any fat off the surface of meat stocks and refrigerate the stock until needed for up to 3 days.

Alternatively, you can freeze the stock in a plastic box or loaf pan lined with a large plastic bag for use later. Seal, label, and freeze for up to 3 months. Defrost at room temperature, or in the microwave if preferred, minus the bag tie if used.

chicken stock

Preparation time **10 minutes**
Cooking time **2–2½ hours**
Makes about **4 cups**

1 leftover **cooked chicken carcass**
1 **onion**, quartered
2 **carrots**, thickly sliced
2 **celery sticks**, thickly sliced
1 **bay leaf** or small bunch of **mixed herbs**
¼ teaspoon **salt**
½ teaspoon roughly crushed **black peppercorns**
2½ quarts **cold water**

Put the chicken carcass and vegetables into a large saucepan. Add the herbs, salt, and peppercorns.
Pour over the water and bring slowly just to a boil. Skim off any scum with a slotted spoon. Reduce the heat to a gentle simmer, then half cover with a lid and cook for 2–2½ hours until reduced by about half.
Strain the stock through a large sieve into a pitcher. Remove any chicken pieces still on the carcass, pick out the meat pieces from the sieve and reserve for the soup, but discard the vegetables. Chill the stock for several hours or overnight.

Skim off the thin layer of fat on the top of the chilled and now jellied stock with a dessertspoon. Chill and store in the refrigerator for up to 3 days.

A duck, pheasant, or guinea fowl carcass or a ham hock can also be made into stock in just the same way. If you have a turkey carcass then double up the vegetable and water quantities specified above.

If you have a chicken carcass but don't have time to make it into stock straightaway, you can freeze it for up to 3 months closely wrapped in plastic wrap, then packed into a plastic bag. Defrost it at room temperature then make into stock as above.

beef stock

Preparation time **10 minutes**
Cooking time **4 hours 20 minutes–
    5 hours 20 minutes**
Makes about **4 cups**

4 lb **beef bones**, such as ribs or shank
2 **bacon slices**, diced
2 **onions**, quartered but with the inner brown
    layer still on
2 **carrots**, thickly sliced
2 **celery sticks**, thickly sliced
1 **turnip**, diced (optional)
2 **bay leaves**, **rosemary sprigs**, or **sage stems**
¼ teaspoon **salt**
½ teaspoon roughly crushed **black
    peppercorns**
3½ quarts **cold water**

Put the bones and bacon into a large
saucepan and heat gently for 10 minutes until
the marrow begins to run from the center of
the bones. Turn the bones occasionally.

Add the vegetables and fry for 10 more
minutes, stirring the vegetables and turning
the bones until browned.

Add the herbs, salt, and peppercorns then
pour in the water and bring slowly to a boil.
Skim off any scum with a slotted spoon, then
reduce the heat, half cover with a lid, and
simmer gently for 4–5 hours until the liquid
has reduced by half.

Strain through a large sieve into a pitcher.
Cool then chill in the refrigerator overnight.
Skim off any fat and store in the refrigerator
for up to 3 days.

If you're not in the habit of roasting large beef
joints on the bone, you can obtain the beef
bones from your local butcher; he may even
give them to you for free. Use the bones raw
when preparing your stock. Lamb stock can
be made in the same way from cooked or
uncooked lamb bones.

fish stock

Preparation time **10 minutes**
Cooking time **45 minutes**
Makes about **4 cups**

2 lb **fish trimmings**, such as heads, backbones, tails, skins, and shrimp shells
1 **onion**, quartered
2 **leek tops**, sliced
2 **carrots**, thickly sliced
2 **celery sticks**, thickly sliced
thyme sprigs
1 **bay leaf**
few **parsley stalks**
½ teaspoon roughly crushed
  white peppercorns
¼ teaspoon **salt**
6 cups **cold water**
1¼ cups **dry white wine** or **extra water**

Put the fish trimmings in a large sieve, rinse with cold water, drain, and then put them into a large saucepan with all the remaining ingredients.
Bring slowly to a boil. Skim off any scum with a slotted spoon. Cover and simmer for 30 minutes.
Strain the stock through a fine sieve, return it to the saucepan and then simmer it, uncovered, for about 15 minutes until reduced by half. Cool then chill in the refrigerator for up to 3 days.

If you are adding fish heads, don't cook them for longer than 30 minutes before straining, or they will begin to add a bitter taste.

vegetable stock

Preparation time **10 minutes**
Cooking time **1 hour 5 minutes**
Makes about **4 cups**

1 tablespoon **olive oil**
2 **onions**, roughly chopped
2 **leek tops**, roughly chopped
4 **carrots**, roughly chopped
2 **celery sticks**, thickly sliced
1½ cups sliced **cup mushrooms**
4 **tomatoes**, roughly chopped
small bunch of **mixed herbs**
½ teaspoon roughly crushed **black**
  peppercorns
¼ teaspoon **salt**
1¾ quarts **cold water**

Heat the oil in a large saucepan, add the vegetables, and fry for 5 minutes until softened and just beginning to turn golden around the edges.
Add the tomatoes, herbs, peppercorns, and salt. Pour in the water, slowly bring to a boil, then half cover and simmer gently for 1 hour.
Pour through a sieve into a pitcher. Cool then chill for up to 3 days.

If you have some opened white wine or hard cider then you can add ⅔ cup wine in place of the same amount of water.

Mix and match vegetables depending on what you have. Chopped fennel or peeled and diced celeriac give a flavorful addition. Half a red or orange bell pepper and a few dried mushrooms are also ideal.

bouillon cubes & ready-made stock

In our grandmothers' day, it would have been unheard of to make soup with a bouillon cube; nowadays, juggling work with family life means that time-saving short-cuts are a must. Very few people make enough stock for all their cooking needs and while it is great to have a few handy-size bags of stock in the freezer, most of us cheat and use store-bought products.

While there is nothing wrong with using bouillon cubes there are some soups for which homemade stock is crucial, such as the light, delicate-tasting Chilled Lettuce Soup (see page 74), Vichysoisse-style soups (see page 64) or clear consommé style broths such as Italian Tortellini in Brodo (see page 208) or Chicken Soup with Lockshen (see page 214). The strength of flavor varies hugely in store-bought bouillon cubes, so choose cubes or powder that are low in salt and make them up with a little extra water so that their flavor is not overpowering.

More and more supermarkets now sell tubs of chilled ready-made stocks and for a special-occasion soup such as Crab Bisque (see page 132) or French Onion Soup (see page 226) they give a much more authentic taste. They are more expensive, but much closer to the taste of homemade stock.

get ahead

Soups make such a warming, satisfying lunch that it is well worthwhile to freeze portions away in individual plastic boxes or plastic bags for occasions when you don't have time to cook from scratch. So, rather than always having a sandwich at work, why not take a frozen pack of soup with you so that it defrosts while you work, then give it a quick blast in the microwave at lunchtime.

If you don't have many plastic boxes, line a rectangular loaf pan with a freezer bag, fill with soup then seal, squeezing out as much air as possible. Freeze until solid then remove the bag from the pan, rinsing with cold water to loosen the bag from the pan if needed. The frozen block then makes for an easy stacking shape in your freezer. Just remember to label and date it, so that you will know what it is when you come to defrost it. There is nothing more frustrating than defrosting an item expecting it to be savory, only to find it is fruit puree or something else sweet instead.

reheating

Only ever reheat foods once. If your family is planning to tuck into a batch of soup at different times, then ladle the amount required at any one time into a smaller saucepan or microwaveable bowl and then reheat thoroughly, leaving the remaining soup in the refrigerator until needed. Don't add extra liquid until the soup is heated through, as many will thin again once hot. Keep a watchful eye on the heat if eggs and cream were used in the recipe; the soup needs to be thoroughly reheated but not boiled rapidly, or the eggs will curdle. Stir frequently so that the soup heats up evenly.

finishing touches

A swirl of cream—this always looks special, yet what could be simpler than to drizzle a tablespoon or two of cream or plain yogurt over a bowlful of pureed soup? Alternatively you can drop small spoonfuls of cream into the soup and then run a toothpick through them for a teardrop effect, or add a spoonful of thick yogurt or crème fraîche into the center of the soup and then sprinkle it with a few snipped herbs.

Herb garnishes—a few finely chopped fresh herbs can be all that is needed to liven up a pale pureed soup, such as fennel vichyssoise. For a crispy herb topping, pan-fry a handful of sage, basil, or parsley leaves for a few seconds. For a topping with punch try a sprinkling of gremolata—a mix of chopped parsley, lemon zest, and chopped garlic—or salsa verde—a mix of chopped herbs, anchovies, garlic, and olive oil. You could make up some herb-infused oil, store in a bottle, and drizzle over the soup at the last minute. Or you can cheat and add a small spoonful of ready-made pesto.

Citrus curls—tiny lemon, lime, or orange curls can be sprinkled over the top of the soup for a delicate zing. Use a zester, or the finest section on a grater.

Spicy sprinkles—try a little freshly grated nutmeg, a few roughly crushed peppercorns, a few dried red pepper flakes for extra heat or a little paprika or turmeric for added color.

Flavored butters and oil—mix a little butter with chopped blue cheese, anchovies, and chili, garlic, lemon zest, or freshly chopped herbs. Shape into a log, chill, slice, and then add a slice to the hot soup just before serving. Alternatively make up some mayonnaise-based sauces and flavor with garlic to make aïoli, chili for rouille, or lemon zest and juice for a citrus burst.

Ice cubes—for chilled soups, add a few whole or roughly crushed ice cubes for added texture and impact.

Croutons—fry diced or sliced bread (half–one slice per serving of soup) in a mixture of butter and sunflower oil or just olive oil until golden. Drain on paper towels and then float on bowls of soup just before serving. Croutons can also be flavored with garlic or spices. For French bread or ciabatta, rub the fried bread with a cut clove of garlic or spread with a little olive tapenade, pesto, or crumbled blue cheese. For a lower-fat option, bake croutons sprayed with a little olive oil in the oven until crisp.

speedy
soups

tomato & balsamic vinegar soup

Serves **6**
Preparation time **25 minutes**
Cooking time **20 minutes**

1½ lb large **tomatoes on the vine**

2 tablespoons **olive oil**

1 **onion**, roughly chopped

1 **baking potato**, about 7 oz, diced

2 **garlic cloves**, finely chopped (optional)

3 cups **vegetable** or **chicken stock** (see pages 13 and 10)

1 tablespoon **tomato paste**

1 tablespoon **brown sugar**

4 teaspoons **balsamic vinegar**

small bunch of **basil**

salt and **pepper**

Cut the tomatoes in half, place them cut-side down in a foil-lined broiler pan and drizzle with some oil. Broil for 4–5 minutes until the skins have split and blackened. Meanwhile, fry the onion, potato, and garlic in the remaining oil for 5 minutes, stirring occasionally until softened and turning golden around the edges.

Peel and roughly chop the tomatoes and add to the onion and potato with the pan juices, then stir in the stock, tomato paste, sugar, and vinegar. Add half the basil, season, and bring to a boil. Cover and simmer for 15 minutes.

Puree half the soup in batches in a blender or food processor until smooth. Return to the saucepan with the rest of the soup and reheat. Season to taste, then ladle into bowls, garnish with the remaining basil leaves, and serve with Parmesan twists.

For Parmesan twists, to serve as an accompaniment, unroll one sheet of ready-rolled puff pastry from a 14 oz defrosted package of 2 sheets. Brush with a little beaten egg yolk then spread with 3 teaspoons tomato (or basil) pesto, a little pepper, and 4 tablespoons of freshly grated Parmesan cheese. Cover with the second unrolled pastry sheet. Brush the top with a little more egg yolk, then cut into strips about ½ inch wide. Twist each strip like a corkscrew, transfer to an oiled baking sheet, and press the ends firmly onto the baking sheet to prevent them unraveling. Cook in a preheated oven, 400°F, for about 10 minutes until golden brown. Serve warm.

black bean with soba noodles

Serves **4**
Preparation time **10 minutes**
Cooking time **15 minutes**

7 oz **dried soba Japanese noodles**
2 tablespoons **peanut** or **vegetable oil**
bunch of **scallions**, sliced
2 **garlic cloves**, roughly chopped
1 **red chili**, seeded and sliced
1½ inch piece of **fresh ginger root**, peeled and grated
½ cup **black bean sauce** or **black bean stir-fry sauce**
3 cups **vegetable stock** (see page 13)
7 oz **bok choy** or **collard greens**, shredded
2 teaspoons **soy sauce**
1 teaspoon **superfine sugar**
¼ cup **raw, unsalted shelled peanuts**

Cook the noodles in a saucepan of boiling water for about 5 minutes, or until just tender.

Meanwhile, heat the oil in a saucepan. Add the scallions and garlic and sauté gently for 1 minute.

Add the red chili, fresh ginger, black bean sauce, and vegetable stock and bring to a boil. Stir in the bok choy or collard greens, soy sauce, superfine sugar, and peanuts; reduce the heat and simmer gently, uncovered, for 4 minutes.

Drain the noodles and pile into serving bowls. Ladle the soup over the noodles and serve immediately.

For beef & black bean soup, reduce the amount of noodles to 4 oz and cook as above. Meanwhile, fry the scallions then add the red chili, ginger, black bean sauce, and stock. Bring to a boil then add the green vegetables, soy sauce, and sugar. Cook for 2 minutes as above. Quickly trim the fat off an 8 oz sirloin steak, cut into thin slices, and add to the soup. Cook for 2 more minutes then ladle into noodle-filled bowls.

fava bean & chorizo soup

Serves **6**
Preparation time **20 minutes**
Cooking time **20 minutes**

2 tablespoons **olive oil**
1 large **onion**, roughly
  chopped
1 lb **potatoes**, diced
5 oz **chorizo**, diced
4 **tomatoes**, diced
1¾ cups **frozen fava beans**
6 cups **chicken stock** (see
  page 10)
salt and **pepper**
basil leaves, to garnish

Olive tapenade toasts
12 slices **French bread**
2 **garlic cloves**, halved
4 tablespoons **green** or **black**
  olive tapenade

Heat the oil in a large saucepan, add the onion, potatoes, and chorizo and fry for 5 minutes, stirring regularly until just beginning to soften.

Stir in the tomatoes, fava beans, and stock, season, and bring to a boil. Cover and simmer for 15 minutes until the vegetables are tender.

Mash some of the potatoes roughly with a fork to thicken the soup slightly. Taste and adjust the seasoning if needed.

Toast the bread on both sides then rub one side with the halves of garlic and spread with the tapenade. Ladle the soup into bowls and top with the tapenade toasts and sprinkle with basil leaves to garnish.

For homemade green olive tapenade, to serve on the toast, pit 1⅓ cups green olives then finely chop them in a food processor with a small bunch of fresh basil, 2 garlic cloves, 2 teaspoons drained capers, 4 tablespoons olive oil, and 1 tablespoon white wine vinegar. This tapenade can also be served with crudités or tossed with pasta. Any remaining tapenade can be stored for up to two weeks in the refrigerator in a small jar with the surface covered with a little extra olive oil.

celeriac & apple soup

Serves **6**

Preparation time **10–15 minutes**

Cooking time **20–25 minutes**

2 tablespoons **butter** or **margarine**

1 **celeriac**, about 1 lb, peeled and coarsely grated

3 **dessert apples**, peeled, cored, and chopped

5 cups **chicken or vegetable stock** (see pages 10 and 13)

pinch of **cayenne pepper**, or more to taste

salt

To garnish

2–3 tablespoons finely diced **dessert apple**

paprika

Melt the butter or margarine in a large saucepan and cook the celeriac and apples over a moderate heat for 5 minutes or until they have begun to soften.

Add the stock and cayenne pepper and bring to a boil. Reduce the heat, cover the pan, and simmer for 15–20 minutes or until the celeriac and apples are very soft.

Puree the mixture in a blender or food processor until it is very smooth, transferring each batch to a clean saucepan. Alternatively, rub through a fine sieve. Reheat gently. Season to taste and serve in individual bowls, garnished with the finely diced apple and a dusting of paprika.

For celeriac & roasted garlic soup, halve 2 garlic bulbs, put into a roasting pan, drizzle with 2 teaspoons olive oil then roast in a preheated oven, 400°F, for 15 minutes. Heat the butter in a saucepan as above, add the celeriac and 1 chopped onion in place of the apples, fry gently for 5 minutes. Take the garlic out of the papery skins, add to the celeriac with 4 cups vegetable stock, salt, and cayenne pepper. Simmer as above. Puree, reheat with 2/3 cup milk then serve swirled with a little cream in each bowl.

broccoli & almond soup

Serves **6**
Preparation time **15 minutes**
Cooking time **15 minutes**

2 tablespoons **butter**
1 **onion**, roughly chopped
1 lb **broccoli**, cut into florets,
  stems sliced
⅓ cup **ground almonds**
3¾ cups **vegetable** or
  chicken stock (see pages
  13 and 10)
1¼ cups **milk**
salt and **pepper**

To garnish
1 tablespoon **butter**
6 tablespoons **plain yogurt**
3 tablespoons **slivered**
  almonds

Heat the butter in a saucepan, add the onion, and fry gently for 5 minutes until just beginning to soften. Stir in the broccoli until coated in the butter then add the ground almonds, stock, and a little salt and pepper.

Bring to a boil then cover and simmer for 10 minutes until the broccoli is just tender and still bright green. Allow to cool slightly, then puree in batches in a blender or food processor until finely speckled with green.

Pour the puree back into the saucepan and stir in the milk. Reheat then taste and adjust the seasoning if needed. Heat 1 tablespoon butter in a skillet, add the almonds and fry for a few minutes, stirring until golden. Ladle the soup into bowls, drizzle a spoonful of yogurt over each bowl, then sprinkle with almonds.

For broccoli & Stilton soup, omit the ground almonds and cook as above, adding 4 oz de-rinded and crumbled Stilton cheese when reheating the soup. Stir until melted, then ladle into bowls and sprinkle with a little extra cheese and some coarsely crushed black pepper.

minestrone

Serves **4**
Preparation time **5 minutes**
Cooking time **23 minutes**

2 tablespoons **olive oil**
1 **onion**, chopped
1 **garlic clove**, crushed
2 **celery sticks**, chopped
1 **leek**, finely sliced
1 **carrot**, chopped
13 oz can **chopped tomatoes**
2½ cups **chicken** or
   vegetable stock (see
   pages 10 and 13)
1 **zucchini**, diced
½ small **cabbage**, shredded
1 **bay leaf**
3 oz **canned navy beans**
3 oz **dried spaghetti**, broken
   into small pieces, or small
   pasta shapes
1 tablespoon chopped
   flat-leaf parsley
salt and **pepper**
grated **Parmesan cheese**,
   to serve

Heat the oil in a large saucepan. Add the onion, garlic, celery, leek, and carrot and cook over a medium heat, stirring occasionally, for 5 minutes. Add the tomatoes, stock, zucchini, cabbage, bay leaf, and navy beans. Bring to a boil, lower the heat, and simmer for 10 minutes.

Add the pasta and season to taste. Stir well and cook for an additional 8 minutes. Keep stirring because the soup may stick to the base of the pan. Just before serving, add the parsley and stir well. Ladle into individual bowls and serve with grated Parmesan.

For minestrone with arugula & basil pesto, make up the soup as above then ladle into bowls. Top with spoonfuls of pesto made by finely chopping ½ cup arugula leaves and ½ cup basil leaves, 1 garlic clove, and 3 tablespoons pine nuts. Mix with 2 tablespoons freshly grated Parmesan, a little salt and pepper, and ½ cup olive oil. Alternatively, put all the pesto ingredients into a blender or food processor and whiz together.

cream of leek & pea soup

Serves **6**
Preparation time **15 minutes**
Cooking time **20 minutes**

2 tablespoons **olive oil**
12 oz **leeks**, slit and well
 washed then thinly sliced
2½ cups **fresh shelled or
 frozen peas**
small bunch of **mint**
3¾ cups **vegetable or
 chicken stock** (see pages
 13 and 10)
⅔ cup **full-fat mascarpone
 cheese**
grated zest of 1 small **lemon**
salt and **pepper**

To garnish
mint leaves (optional)
lemon zest curls (optional)

Heat the oil in a saucepan, add the leeks, toss in the oil, then cover and fry gently for 10 minutes, stirring occasionally, until softened but not browned. Mix in the peas and cook briefly.

Pour the stock into the pan, add a little salt and pepper then bring to a boil. Cover and simmer gently for 10 minutes.

Ladle half the soup into a blender or food processor, add all the mint, and blend until smooth. Pour the puree back into the saucepan. Mix the mascarpone with half of the lemon zest, reserving the rest for a garnish. Spoon half the mixture into the soup, then reheat, stirring until the mascarpone has melted. Taste and adjust the seasoning if needed. Ladle the soup into bowls, top with spoonfuls of the remaining mascarpone and a sprinkling of the remaining lemon zest. Garnish with mint leaves and lemon zest curls, if desired.

For cream of leek, pea, & watercress soup, use just 1¼ cups peas and add a roughly chopped bunch of watercress. Simmer in 2½ cups of stock then, instead of adding the mascarpone, stir in ⅔ cup milk and ⅔ cup heavy cream, drizzling a little extra cream over at the end and topping with some crispy broiled and chopped bacon to garnish.

chili, bean, & pepper soup

Serves **6**

Preparation time **20 minutes**

Cooking time **30 minutes**

2 tablespoons **sunflower oil**

1 large **onion**, finely chopped

4 **garlic cloves**, finely chopped

2 **red bell peppers**, cored, seeded, and diced

2 **red chilies**, seeded and finely chopped

3¾ cups **vegetable stock** (see page 13)

3 cups **tomato juice** or **passata (sieved tomatoes)**

1 tablespoon **tomato paste**

1 tablespoon **sundried tomato paste**

2 tablespoons **sweet chili sauce**

13 oz can **red kidney beans**, drained

2 tablespoons finely chopped **cilantro**

salt and **pepper**

5 tablespoons **sour cream**, plus extra for serving (optional)

Heat the oil in a large saucepan and fry the onion and garlic until soft but not browned. Stir in the peppers and chilies and fry for a few minutes. Stir in the stock and tomato juice or passata, the tomato pastes, chili sauce, kidney beans, and cilantro. Bring to a boil, cover the pan, and simmer for 20 minutes.

Cool slightly, then puree in a blender or food processor until smooth. Alternatively, rub through a sieve. Return the soup to the pan and adjust the seasoning, adding a little extra chili sauce if necessary. Bring to a boil and serve in individual bowls. Stir a little sour cream into each portion and serve with tortilla chips, extra sour cream and lime zest, if desired.

For chili, eggplant, & pepper soup, heat 2 tablespoons sunflower oil in a saucepan, add 1 diced eggplant along with the onion and garlic, fry until the eggplant is very lightly browned then add the peppers and chilies. Add 2½ cups stock then the tomato juice, tomato pastes, and chili sauce. Omit the red kidney beans and add a small bunch of basil instead. Simmer then puree as above and adjust the consistency if needed with a little extra stock.

stracciatella

Serves **6**
Preparation time **5 minutes**
Cooking time **4–6 minutes**

5 cups **chicken stock** (see
    page 10)
4 **eggs**
¼ cup freshly grated
    Parmesan cheese, plus
    extra to serve
2 tablespoons **fresh white
    bread crumbs**
¼ teaspoon **grated nutmeg**
salt and **pepper**
basil leaves

Pour the stock into a saucepan and bring to a boil.
Reduce the heat and simmer for 2–3 minutes. Beat
the eggs, Parmesan, bread crumbs, and nutmeg in
a bowl and season generously. Gradually beat
2 ladlefuls of hot stock into the eggs.

Reduce the heat under the saucepan then slowly stir
the egg mixture into the stock until smooth, making
sure that the temperature remains moderate, as the
egg will curdle if the soup boils. Gently simmer for
2–3 minutes until piping hot.

Tear the basil leaves into pieces and add to the pan,
then ladle the soup into bowls. Serve with extra
Parmesan to grate over the soup to taste.

For egg drop soup, heat 5 cups of chicken stock as
above, then add ½ teaspoon of superfine sugar and
1 tablespoon of soy sauce. Beat 2 eggs together
in a small bowl. Stir the stock with a fork in a circular
motion, then drizzle the beaten egg through the
prongs of the fork held high over the soup so that it
sets in droplets in the swirling stock. Leave for a
minute or two until the egg has set, then ladle into
bowls. Garnish with sliced green scallion tops and
a little chopped cilantro or green chili.

zucchini soup with gremolata

Serves **6**
Preparation time **15 minutes**
Cooking time **25 minutes**

2 tablespoons **butter**
1 **onion**, finely chopped
½ cup diced **zucchini**
1 **celery stick**, diced
2 **garlic cloves**, finely
   chopped
6 tablespoons **arborio rice**
5 cups **chicken** or **vegetable
   stock** (see pages 10
   and 13)
⅔ cup **dry white wine**
2 **eggs**, beaten
4 tablespoons freshly grated
   Parmesan cheese
salt and **pepper**

Gremolata
small bunch of **basil**
small bunch of **parsley**
2 teaspoons **capers**
grated zest of **1 lemon**

Heat the butter in a saucepan, add the onion, and fry gently for 5 minutes until softened. Stir in the zucchini, celery, and garlic and fry briefly, then stir in the rice.

Pour in the stock and wine, season with salt and pepper, and simmer for 15 minutes, stirring occasionally until the rice is tender.

Take the pan off the heat and allow to cool slightly. Beat the eggs and Parmesan together in a bowl, then gradually mix in a ladleful of the hot stock. Pour this mixture back into the saucepan and stir well. Heat gently until the soup has thickened slightly but do not boil or the eggs will scramble.

Chop all the gremolata ingredients finely and mix together. Ladle the soup into bowls and sprinkle with the gremolata.

For zucchini, lemon, & salmon soup, make up the soup as above, adding 12 oz salmon steak for the last 10 minutes of the soup's cooking time. Lift out and flake the fish into pieces discarding the skin and any bones. Beat 2 eggs with the juice of ½ lemon in a bowl, gradually mix in a ladleful of the hot soup then stir back into the saucepan. Heat gently until the soup is slightly thickened. Divide the salmon between serving bowls, ladle the soup on top, and sprinkle with a little parsley.

pea, lettuce, & lemon soup

Serves **4**
Preparation time **10 minutes**
Cooking time **15–20 minutes**

2 tablespoons **butter**
1 large **onion**, finely chopped
3 cups **frozen peas**
2 small **crisphead lettuces**,
  roughly chopped
4 cups **vegetable** or **chicken
  stock** (see pages 13
  and 10)
grated zest and juice of
  ½ **lemon**
salt and **pepper**

Sesame croutons
2 thick slices of **bread**, cubed
1 tablespoon **olive oil**
1 tablespoon **sesame seeds**

Brush the bread cubes with the oil and put in a roasting pan. Sprinkle with the sesame seeds and bake in a preheated oven, 400°F, for 10–15 minutes, or until golden.

Meanwhile, heat the butter in a large saucepan and fry the onion for 5 minutes until softened. Add the peas, lettuce, stock, lemon zest and juice, and salt and pepper to taste. Bring to a boil, then reduce the heat, cover the pan, and simmer for 10–15 minutes.

Allow the soup to cool slightly, then transfer to a blender or food processor and whiz until smooth. Return the soup to the pan, adjust the seasoning if necessary, and heat through. Spoon into warmed serving bowls and sprinkle with the sesame croutons.

For pea, spinach, & lemon soup, make up the soup as above adding 2½ cups young leaf spinach instead of the lettuces. Simmer for 10–15 minutes then puree. Reheat and add a little grated nutmeg to taste. Ladle into bowls and top with 2 teaspoons plain yogurt per serving.

garden herb soup

Serves **4**
Preparation time **15 minutes**
Cooking time **30 minutes**

¼ cup **butter**
1 **onion**, roughly chopped
1 **baking potato**, about 8 oz,
  diced
4 cups **ham**, **chicken**, or
  vegetable stock
  (see pages 10 and 13)
2 cups **mixed parsley** and
  chives, roughly torn
  into pieces
salt and **pepper**

Heat the butter in a saucepan, add the onion, and fry gently for 5 minutes until softened but not browned. Add the potato, toss in the butter, then cover and fry gently for 10 minutes, stirring occasionally until just turning golden around the edges.

Add the stock, season with salt and pepper, and bring to a boil. Cover and simmer for 10 minutes or until the potatoes are tender. Cool slightly then puree in batches in a blender or food processor with the herbs.

Pour back into the saucepan, reheat, then taste and adjust the seasoning if needed. Serve in mugs with toasted bacon sandwiches.

For Italian herb soup, heat 2 tablespoons of olive oil in a pan, add the onion and fry until softened. Mix in ¾ cup diced potato, cover, and fry for 10 minutes. Mix in the stock and seasoning as above, cover, and simmer for 10 minutes. Puree the soup in the blender, replacing the parsley and chives with 2 cups arugula leaves, and adding ¼ cup ground pine nuts or almonds and ⅓ cup freshly grated Parmesan. Reheat and serve topped with toasted pine nuts.

red chicken & coconut broth

Serves **4**
Preparation time **10 minutes**
Cooking time **20–21 minutes**

1 tablespoon **sunflower oil**
8 oz boned and skinned
chicken thighs, diced
4 teaspoons **ready-made red Thai curry paste**
1 teaspoon **ready-made galangal paste**
3 dried **kaffir lime leaves**
1¾ cups **full-fat coconut milk**
2 teaspoons **Thai fish sauce**
1 teaspoon **light brown sugar**
2½ cups **chicken stock** (see page 10)
4 **scallions**, thinly sliced, plus 2 extra to garnish
¾ cup **snow peas**, sliced
1 cup **bean sprouts**, rinsed
small bunch of **cilantro leaves**

Heat the oil in a saucepan, add the chicken and curry paste, and fry for 3–4 minutes until just beginning to brown. Stir in the galangal paste, lime leaves, coconut milk, fish sauce, and brown sugar, then mix in the stock.

Bring to a boil, cover, and simmer for 15 minutes, stirring occasionally until the chicken is cooked.

Create curls by cutting very thin strips from the two scallions reserved for a garnish. Soak in cold water for 10 minutes, then drain.

Add the remaining scallions, snow peas, and bean sprouts and cook for 2 minutes. Ladle into bowls and tear the cilantro leaves over the top. Sprinkle the scallion curls over the soup.

For red fish & coconut broth, heat the oil, add the curry paste, and fry for 1 minute. Add the galangal paste, lime leaves, coconut milk, fish sauce, and brown sugar. Pour in the stock then add an 8 oz salmon fillet. Cover and simmer for 10 minutes, lift out the fish and flake it into pieces, discarding the skin and bones. Return the salmon to the broth, add the vegetables and 4 oz small shrimp, defrosted and rinsed if frozen. Cook for 2 minutes then serve with the cilantro leaves as above.

shrimp & noodle soup

Serves **4**
Preparation time **10 minutes**
Cooking time **15 minutes**

3¾ cups **vegetable** or
   chicken stock (see pages
   13 and 10)
2 dried **kaffir lime leaves**
1 **lemon grass stalk**, lightly
   bruised
5 oz **dried egg noodles**
⅓ cup **frozen peas**
⅓ cup **frozen corn**
4 large **jumbo shrimp**,
   cooked, peeled, and
   deveined, or defrosted if
   frozen, rinsed with cold
   water and drained
4 **scallions**, sliced
2 teaspoons **soy sauce**

Put the stock into a saucepan with the lime leaves and lemon grass, bring to a boil, then reduce the heat and simmer for 10 minutes.

Add the noodles to the stock and cook according to the package instructions. After 2 minutes, add the peas, corn, prawns, scallions, and soy sauce and cook for 2 more minutes. Remove and discard the lemon grass. Serve the soup in warmed bowls.

For chicken & noodle soup, put the stock, lime leaves, and lemon grass into a saucepan then add 2 boneless, skinless, chicken breasts that have been diced, bring to a boil, then simmer for 10 minutes. Continue as above.

44

cream of corn soup

Serves **4–6**

Preparation time **5–10 minutes**

Cooking time about **25–30 minutes**

3 tablespoons **butter**
1 **onion**, chopped
2 **potatoes**, diced
¼ cup **all-purpose flour**
3¾ cups **milk**
1 **bay leaf**
2 x 11 oz cans **corn**, drained
6 tablespoons **heavy cream**
salt and **pepper**
fried **bacon**, crumbled, to garnish

Melt the butter in a large saucepan. Add the onion and potatoes and cook over a low heat, stirring frequently, for 5 minutes, without browning.

Stir in the flour, then gradually add the milk, stirring constantly. Bring to a boil, add the bay leaf, and season to taste with salt and pepper. Add half the corn, cover the pan, and simmer for 15–20 minutes.

Remove and discard the bay leaf and set the soup aside to cool slightly. Puree the soup in a blender or food processor or rub it through a sieve until smooth. Return it to the pan, add the remaining corn, and heat through.

Stir in the cream, sprinkle with the bacon, and serve the soup immediately.

For cream of sweet potato & corn soup, fry the onion in the butter as above, add 2 cups diced sweet potato instead of the ordinary potatoes then continue as above. Serve the soup with a little diced and fried chorizo sausage instead of the bacon.

mediterranean garlic soup

Serves **4**

Preparation time **10 minutes**

Cooking time **16–18 minutes**

2 tablespoons **olive oil**

2–3 **garlic cloves**, finely chopped

4 oz **chorizo**, diced

6 tablespoons **red wine**

4 cups **beef stock** (see page 12) or **game stock**

2 teaspoons **tomato paste**

1 teaspoon **brown sugar**

4 **eggs**

salt and **pepper**

parsley, chopped, to garnish

Heat the oil in a saucepan, add the garlic and chorizo, and fry gently for 3–4 minutes. Add the wine, stock, tomato paste, and sugar, season with salt and pepper, and simmer for 5 minutes.

Reduce the heat to a very gentle simmer then drop the eggs one at a time into the liquid, leaving space between them. Poach for 3–4 minutes until the whites are set and the yolks set to your taste.

Taste and adjust the seasoning if needed, then ladle an egg into the base of each serving bowl, cover with the soup, and sprinkle with a little chopped parsley. Serve with diced croutons (see page 15).

For garlic & potato soup, add 1¾ cups diced potato when frying the onion and chorizo. Add the wine, stock, tomato paste, sugar, and seasoning and simmer for 30 minutes. Ladle the soup into bowls and serve with garlic croutes topped with grated Gruyère cheese (see page 226).

hot & sour soup

Serves **4**
Preparation time **10 minutes**
Cooking time **12 minutes**

3 cups **vegetable** or **fish
stock** (see page 13)
4 dried **kaffir lime leaves**
1 inch piece **fresh ginger
root**, peeled and grated
1 **red chili**, seeded and sliced
1 **lemon grass stalk**, lightly
bruised
4 oz **mushrooms**, sliced
4 oz **rice noodles**
2 cups **baby spinach**
4 oz cooked, peeled **jumbo
shrimp**, or defrosted if
frozen, rinsed with cold
water and drained
2 tablespoons **lemon juice**
freshly ground **black pepper**

Put the stock, lime leaves, fresh ginger root, chili,
and lemon grass in a large saucepan. Cover and
bring to a boil. Add the mushrooms and simmer for
2 minutes. Break the noodles into short lengths, drop
into the soup, and simmer for 3 minutes.

Add the baby spinach and shrimp and simmer for
2 minutes until the shrimp are heated through. Add the
lemon juice. Remove and discard the lemon grass stalk
and season the soup with black pepper before serving.

For hot coconut soup, make up the soup as above,
adding just 1¾ cups stock and 1¾ cups coconut
milk, plus 2 teaspoons ready-made Thai red curry
paste. Continue as above and serve sprinkled with a
little chopped cilantro.

cheesy cauliflower & cider soup

Serves **6**

Preparation time **15 minutes**

Cooking time **30 minutes**

3 tablespoons **butter**

1 **onion**, finely chopped

1⅓ cups coarsely grated **potato**

1 **cauliflower**, cut into small florets, woody core discarded, about 2 cups when prepared

3¾ cups **chicken** or **vegetable stock** (see pages 10 and 13)

1¼ cups **hard cider**

2 teaspoons **wholegrain mustard**

¾ cup grated **sharp cheddar cheese**

salt and **cayenne pepper**

chopped chives, to garnish

Heat the butter in a saucepan, add the onion, and fry gently for 5 minutes until just beginning to turn golden around the edges. Stir in the potato and cook briefly, then mix in the cauliflower florets, stock, cider, and mustard. Season with salt and pepper and bring to a boil. Cover and simmer for 15 minutes until the vegetables are tender.

Mash the soup roughly to thicken it slightly, then stir in the cheese and heat, stirring until melted. Taste and adjust the seasoning if needed, then ladle into bowls. Garnish with chopped chives and serve with croutons (see page 15) or Welsh rarebit toasts.

For Welsh rarebit toasts, to serve as an accompaniment, mix 1 cup grated sharp cheddar with 1 egg yolk, 2 teaspoons Worcestershire sauce, 1 teaspoon wholegrain mustard, and a little cayenne pepper. Toast 4 slices of bread lightly on both sides. Spread the cheese mixture over the top of each then cook under a hot broiler until the cheese is bubbling and golden. Cut into thin strips to serve.

chilled
soups

beet & apple soup

Serves **6**

Preparation time **25 minutes**

Cooking time **50 minutes**,
plus chilling

1 tablespoon **olive oil**

1 **onion**, roughly chopped

1 lb bunch of uncooked **beet**,
trimmed, peeled, and diced

1 large **cooking apple**, about
12 oz, quartered, cored,
peeled, and diced

6 cups **vegetable** or **chicken
stock** (see pages 13
and 10)

salt and **pepper**

To finish

6 tablespoons **sour cream**

1 **red dessert apple**, cored
and diced

seeds from ½ **pomegranate**

4 tablespoons **maple syrup**

Heat the oil in a saucepan, add the onion, and fry gently for 5 minutes until softened. Add the beet and apple, pour in the stock, season with salt and pepper, and bring to a boil. Cover and simmer for 45 minutes, stirring occasionally until the beet is tender.

Allow the soup to cool slightly, then puree in batches in a blender or food processor until smooth. Pour into a large pitcher, taste and adjust the seasoning if needed, then chill in the refrigerator for 3–4 hours or overnight.

Pour the soup into bowls to serve and top with a spoonful of sour cream, sprinkle with the diced apple and pomegranate seeds, then drizzle with a little maple syrup. Serve extra maple syrup in a small pitcher to add as required and accompany with sliced rye bread, if desired.

For beet & orange soup, fry the onion in oil as above, add the beet (omit the apple) and simmer with the stock and a little salt and pepper for 45 minutes. Puree the soup as above and mix with the grated zest and juice of 2 large oranges. Chill and serve with a swirl of cream, a drizzle of honey, and some orange-zest curls made with a zester.

chilled melon foam

Serves **6**
Preparation time **15 minutes**

2 ripe **Galia** or **cantaloupe melons**
freshly squeezed **juice of 1 lime**
½–1 large **mild red chili**, seeded and quartered
small bunch of **cilantro**, plus extra sprigs to garnish
1¼ cups pressed **apple juice**
lime wedges, to garnish (optional)

Cut the melons in half, scoop out and discard the seeds, then scoop the flesh away from the skin and put it into a blender or food processor with the lime juice, chili, and cilantro, torn into pieces. Add half the apple juice and blend until smooth. Gradually mix in the remaining juice until frothy.

Pour the soup into cups or glass tumblers half filled with ice and serve immediately, garnished with a sprig of cilantro and lime wedges if desired, before the foamy texture loses its bubbles.

For gingered melon foam, scoop out the flesh from 2 halved, seeded, charentais melons, then puree with 2 chopped scallions and ⅔ cup low-fat sour cream in a blender or food processor. Add ⅔ cup ginger ale and puree until frothy. Pour into shallow bowls or back into the empty melon shells to serve.

sour cherry soup

Serves **6**

Preparation time **10 minutes**

Cooking time **12 minutes**,
   plus chilling

1¼ cups **white Riesling wine**

1¾ cups **water**

2 tablespoons **superfine
   sugar**

1 **cinnamon stick**, halved

grated **zest** and **juice** of
   1 **lemon**

2 cups **frozen pitted cherries**

1¼ cups **sour cream**

ground cinnamon, to garnish

Pour the wine and water into a saucepan, add the sugar, cinnamon stick, and lemon zest and juice. Bring to a boil and simmer for 5 minutes.

Add the still-frozen cherries and simmer for 5 minutes. Discard the cinnamon stick, then ladle half the liquid and cherries into a blender or food processor. Add the sour cream and then blend, in batches if needed, until smooth. Return the blended liquid to the saucepan and mix well.

Chill the soup thoroughly, then ladle into shallow bowls so that the whole cherries can be seen and sprinkle with a little ground cinnamon to garnish. Serve with some cherries on stalks, if desired.

For peppered strawberry soup, make up the syrup as above with the wine, water, sugar, and lemon zest and juice, adding ½ teaspoon crushed colored peppercorns in place of the cinnamon. Simmer for 5 minutes then add 3 cups sliced or halved strawberries depending on their size. Finish the soup as above.

avocado & sour cream soup

Serves **6**
Preparation time **15 minutes**
Cooking time **5 minutes**

1 tablespoon **sunflower oil**
4 **scallions**, sliced, plus
  2 extra to garnish
2 large ripe **avocados**, halved
  and pitted
4 tablespoons **sour cream**
2½ cups **vegetable** or
  chicken stock (see pages
  13 and 10)
juice of 2 **limes**
salt and **pepper**
Tabasco sauce

Heat the oil in a skillet, add the scallions, and fry for 5 minutes until softened. Cut very thin strips from the remaining scallions to create curls. Soak in cold water for 10 minutes, then drain.

Scoop out the avocado flesh from the shells with a dessertspoon and add to a blender or food processor with the fried scallions, the sour cream, and about a third of the stock. Blend until a smooth puree, then gradually mix in the remaining stock and lime juice. Season to taste with salt, pepper, and a few drops of Tabasco sauce.

Serve the soup immediately while the avocado is still bright green in cups or glass tumblers containing some ice. Scatter the scallion curls over the soup and serve with breadsticks or grissini.

For homemade salt & pepper grissini, to serve as an accompaniment, put 1½ cups white bread flour into a bowl and mix with ¼ teaspoon salt, 1 teaspoon superfine sugar, and 1 teaspoon instant yeast. Add 4 teaspoons olive oil and gradually mix in up to ⅔ cup warm water until you've made a smooth dough. Knead for 5 minutes on a lightly floured surface, then cut the dough into 18 pieces and roll each into a thin rope. Put these on a greased baking sheet, cover with oiled plastic wrap, and leave in a warm place to rise for 30 minutes. Remove the plastic wrap, brush the bread with beaten egg, then sprinkle with a little coarse sea salt and a generous sprinkling of roughly crushed black peppercorns. Bake in a preheated oven, 400°F, for 6–8 minutes until golden. Serve warm or cold with the soup.

fennel vichyssoise

Serves **6**
Preparation time **20 minutes**
Cooking time **30 minutes**,
　plus chilling

2 tablespoons **butter**
1 **fennel bulb**, about 7–8 oz,
　green feathery tops trimmed
　and reserved, core
　discarded, bulb roughly
　chopped
4 **scallions**, thickly sliced
¾ cup diced **potato**
1¾ cups **chicken stock** (see
　page 10)
1 cup **milk**
⅔ cup **heavy cream**
salt and **pepper**

Heat the butter in a saucepan, add the chopped fennel, scallions, and potato, toss in the butter then cover and fry gently for 10 minutes, stirring occasionally until softened but not browned.

Pour in the stock, season, and bring to a boil. Cover and simmer for 15 minutes until the vegetables are just tender and still tinged green.

Allow the soup to cool slightly, then puree in batches in a blender or food processor until smooth. Pour the puree through a fine sieve back into the saucepan, then press the coarser pieces of fennel through the sieve using the back of a ladle. Mix in the milk and cream, then taste and adjust the seasoning if needed. Chill well.

Ladle the soup into small bowls or glasses half filled with ice and garnish with the reserved green feathery tops, snipped into small pieces.

For classic vichyssoise, omit the fennel and scallions and add instead 12 oz leeks that have been slit, rinsed well in cold water then drained and sliced. Stir half the cream into the soup and swirl the rest through the bowls before serving. Garnish with a sprinkling of a few snipped chives.

gazpacho

Serves **6**

Preparation time **10–15 minutes**, plus chilling

2 **garlic cloves**, roughly chopped

¼ teaspoon **salt**

3 slices of **thick white bread**, crusts removed

12 oz **tomatoes**, skinned and coarsely chopped

½ large **cucumber**, peeled, seeded, and coarsely chopped

1 large **red bell pepper**, cored, seeded, and coarsely chopped

2 **celery sticks**, quartered

5 tablespoons **olive oil**

4 tablespoons **white wine vinegar**

4 cups **water**

freshly ground **black pepper**

To garnish

2 **tomatoes**, seeded and diced

¼ **cucumber**, diced

½ **red onion**, finely chopped

Combine the chopped garlic and salt in a mortar and pound with a pestle until smooth. Alternatively, place the garlic and salt on a board and crush the garlic with the flattened blade of a knife. Place the bread in a bowl and cover with cold water. Soak for 5 seconds, then drain the bread and squeeze out the moisture.

Place the tomatoes, cucumber, pepper, and celery in a blender or food processor. Add the garlic paste, bread, and oil and puree the mixture until very smooth.

Pour the mixture into a large bowl and stir in the vinegar and water and add pepper to taste. Cover closely and chill in the refrigerator for at least 3 hours. Serve the soup very cold in individual chilled glasses. Garnish with a sprinkling of the diced tomatoes, cucumber, and red onion.

For chilied gazpacho, make up the soup as above, adding 1 large, mild, seeded and finely chopped red chili along with the other vegetables. Serve garnished with a sprinkling of finely chopped mint and a drizzle of olive oil.

chilled almond & grape soup

Serves **6**

Preparation time **20 minutes**, plus chilling

4 oz stale **ciabatta bread**, crusts removed

2½ cups **chicken stock** (see page 10)

⅔ cup **blanched almonds**

1–2 **garlic cloves**, sliced

2 tablespoons **olive oil**

2 tablespoons **sherry vinegar**

salt and **pepper**

To garnish

3 tablespoons **slivered almonds**, toasted

1 cup **seedless grapes**, halved

Tear the bread into pieces into a bowl, pour over ⅔ cup of the stock and allow to soak for 5 minutes until softened.

Grind the almonds and garlic together in a food processor or blender until they form a fine powder then add the soaked bread with its stock, the oil, vinegar, and a little salt and pepper. Blend together then gradually mix in the remaining stock.

Chill for at least 2 hours. Taste and adjust the seasoning if needed, then ladle into small bowls and sprinkle with the grapes and slivered almonds to garnish. Serve with fresh ciabatta.

For chilled tomato & almond soup, make up the soup as above, soaking the bread in ⅔ cup stock then mixing in 1¾ cups extra stock along with ⅔ cup passata (sieved tomatoes). Chill well and garnish with toasted slivered almonds, 4 pieces sundried tomato in oil, and some basil leaves in place of the grapes.

bloody mary soup

Serves **6**
Preparation time **20 minutes**
Cooking time **25 minutes**,
  plus chilling

1 tablespoon **olive oil**, plus
  extra to serve
1 **onion**, chopped
1 **red bell pepper**, cored,
  seeded, and diced
2 **celery sticks**, sliced
1 lb **plum tomatoes**, chopped
3¾ cups **vegetable stock**
  (see page 13)
2 teaspoons **superfine sugar**
4 teaspoons **Worcestershire
  sauce**
4 teaspoons **tomato paste**
4 tablespoons **vodka**
few drops of **Tabasco sauce**
salt and **pepper**
baby **celery sticks with
  leaves**, to garnish

Heat the oil in a saucepan, add the onion, and fry for
5 minutes until softened but not browned. Stir in the
red pepper, celery, and tomatoes and fry for 5 minutes,
stirring occasionally.

Pour in the stock, add the sugar, Worcestershire sauce,
tomato paste, and a little salt and pepper and bring to a
boil. Cover and simmer for 15 minutes.

Allow the soup to cool slightly, then puree in batches
in a blender or food processor until smooth. Sieve if
desired then pour back into the saucepan. Add the
vodka and Tabasco to taste, and adjust the seasoning
if needed. Chill well.

Ladle the soup into small bowls or glasses, add tiny
celery sticks, drizzle with a little extra olive oil, and
sprinkle with a little extra pepper.

For virgin mary & pesto soup, fry the onion in the oil
as above, add the red pepper, celery, and tomatoes,
then simmer in 3¾ cups stock mixed with 4 teaspoons
sundried tomato paste and 2 teaspoons superfine
sugar for 15 minutes. Puree with 1 tablespoon pesto.
Chill and serve with a little extra pesto added to each
bowl and garnished with a few tiny basil leaves.

yogurt, walnut, & cucumber soup

Serves **4**

Preparation time **15 minutes**, plus soaking and chilling

½ **cucumber**

3 tablespoons **walnut pieces**

1 **garlic clove**

4 stems **dill weed**

½ slice **white bread**, torn into pieces

2 tablespoons **olive oil**

1¾ cups **low-fat plain yogurt**

4 tablespoons **cold water**

2 teaspoons **lemon juice**

salt and **pepper**

To garnish

little extra **olive oil**

few chopped **walnuts**

dill sprigs

Peel off half the cucumber skin, then roughly chop the cucumber. Put it onto a plate and sprinkle with a little salt. Set aside for 20 minutes.

Rinse the cucumber with cold water and drain well in a sieve. Put the walnuts, garlic, dill, bread, and oil into a blender or food processor and whiz until finely chopped. Add the cucumber and yogurt and blend again until the cucumber is finely chopped. Mix in the water, lemon juice, and season with salt and pepper to taste. Chill well.

Ladle into glasses. Drizzle the top with a little extra olive oil, sprinkle with a few walnuts and a sprig or two of dill. Serve with strips of toasted pita bread, if desired.

For minted yogurt, almond, & cucumber soup, salt the cucumber as above. Omit the walnuts, garlic, and dill weed, adding ¼ cup ground almonds and 2 stems fresh mint in their place. Blend with the bread and oil as above, then add the rinsed and drained cucumber, yogurt, water, lemon juice, and season with salt and pepper. Blend again, then chill. Ladle into bowls and garnish with a swirl of olive oil, a few toasted slivered almonds, and some tiny mint leaves.

chilled lettuce soup

Serves **6**

Preparation time **15 minutes**

Cooking time **14–15 minutes**, plus chilling

2 tablespoons **butter**

4 **scallions**, sliced

1⅔ cups **shelled fresh** or **frozen peas**

1 **Romaine lettuce heart**, leaves separated, rinsed

2½ cups **chicken** or **vegetable stock** (see pages 10 and 13)

1 teaspoon **superfine sugar**

6 tablespoons **heavy cream**

salt and **pepper**

To serve

12 **crisphead lettuce leaves**

1 small fresh prepared **crab on the shell**, about 5 oz

2 tablespoons **mayonnaise**

1 tablespoon **lemon juice**

little **paprika**

Heat the butter in a saucepan, add the scallions, and fry for 2–3 minutes until softened. Add the peas, cook for 2 minutes, then shred and add the lettuce. Pour over the stock, add the sugar and a little salt and pepper, and bring to a boil.

Cover and simmer gently for 10 minutes until the lettuce is wilted but still bright green. Allow to cool slightly, then puree in batches in a blender or food processor until smooth. Stir in the cream, then taste and adjust the seasoning if needed. Chill well.

Ladle the soup into small bowls set on plates. Serve with crisphead lettuce leaves topped with a small amount of crab mixed with the mayonnaise and lemon juice, and sprinkled with paprika.

For chilled watercress soup, heat the butter as above, slice 1 small leek, add the white slices and 1 cup diced potato, cover, and fry gently for 10 minutes, stirring occasionally. Add 3 cups chicken or vegetable stock, season, then cover and simmer for 10 minutes. Add the green leek tops, 2 bunches or 7 oz watercress, cover, and cook for 5 minutes until the watercress is just wilted. Puree in batches as above, then return to the pan and mix with ⅔ cup milk and ⅔ cup heavy cream. Chill well. Serve in shallow bowls with a swirl of cream.

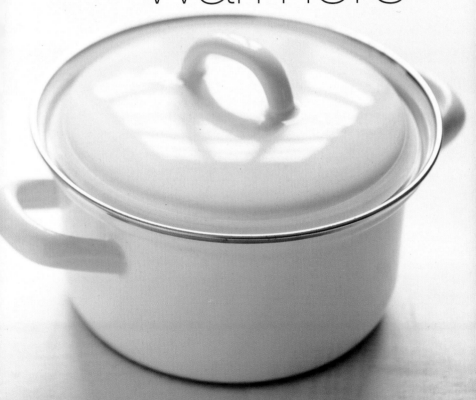

winter warmers

smoked eggplant & tomato soup

Serves **6**
Preparation time **20 minutes**
Cooking time **60 minutes**

2 large **eggplants**
2 tablespoons **olive oil**
1 large **onion**, roughly
    chopped
2 **garlic cloves**, finely
    chopped
1 lb **plum tomatoes**, skinned
    and chopped
½ teaspoon **smoked paprika**
1 teaspoon **superfine sugar**
2½ cups **vegetable** or
    chicken stock (see pages
    13 and 10)
salt and **pepper**

Anchovy toasts
2 oz can **anchovy fillets in oil**,
    drained, finely chopped
2 tablespoons **chopped
    chives**
⅓ cup **butter**
1 small **baguette** or ½ **French
    stick**, sliced

Prick each eggplant just below the stalk and cook under a hot broiler for 15 minutes, turning several times until the skin is blistered and blackened. Transfer to a cutting board and allow to cool.

Heat the oil in a large saucepan, add the onion, and fry, stirring, for 5 minutes until softened. Meanwhile, cut the eggplants in half and use a spoon to scoop out the soft flesh, leaving the blackened skin behind.

Add the eggplant flesh and garlic to the onion and fry for 2 minutes. Mix in the tomatoes, smoked paprika, and sugar and cook briefly, then stir in the stock and season with salt and pepper. Bring to a boil, cover, and simmer for 30 minutes.

Puree the soup in batches in a blender or food processor until smooth. Pour back into the saucepan and reheat. Mix together the anchovies, chives, butter, and a little pepper. Toast the bread and spread with the anchovy butter. Ladle the soup into bowls and float the anchovy toasts on top. Serve immediately.

For smoked tomato soup, omit the eggplants and add 1¾ lb skinned and chopped tomatoes to the fried onion and garlic. Flavor with smoked paprika as above then simmer with the stock, sugar, and salt and pepper. Serve the pureed soup with a drizzle of chilied olive oil instead of the anchovy toasts.

spiced lamb & sweet potato soup

Serves **6**
Preparation time **30 minutes**
Cooking time **2½ hours**

1 tablespoon **olive oil**
1 lb **stewing lamb on the bone**
1 **onion**, finely chopped
1–2 **garlic cloves**, finely chopped
2 teaspoons **ras el hanout Moroccan spice blend**
1 inch piece **fresh ginger root**, grated
8 cups **lamb** or **chicken stock** (see pages 12 and 10)
6 tablespoons **red lentils**
1¼ cups diced **sweet potato**
1 cup diced **carrot**
salt and **pepper**
small bunch of **cilantro**, to garnish (optional)

Heat the oil in a large saucepan, add the lamb, and fry until browned on one side, turn it over and add the onion. Cook until the lamb is browned all over and the onion just beginning to brown.

Stir in the garlic, spice blend, and ginger, then the stock, lentils, and salt and pepper. Bring to a boil then reduce the heat, cover, and simmer for 1½ hours.

Add the sweet potato and carrot, bring back to a simmer then re-cover and cook for 1 hour. Lift the lamb out of the soup with a draining spoon, put onto a plate then carefully remove bones and excess fat, breaking the meat into small pieces. Return the meat to the pan and reheat if needed. Taste and adjust the seasoning if needed.

Ladle the soup into bowls, sprinkle with torn cilantro leaves, and serve with hot fennel flat breads.

For homemade fennel flat breads, to serve as an accompaniment, put 1¾ cups self-rising flour and ½ teaspoon baking powder into a bowl. Add 1 teaspoon fennel seeds that have been roughly crushed using a mortar and pestle and a little salt and pepper. Add 2 tablespoons olive oil, then gradually mix in 6–7 tablespoons of water to make a soft dough. Cut the dough into 6 pieces, then roll each piece out on a lightly floured surface until a rough oval shape about the size of a hand. Cook on a preheated ridged skillet for 3–4 minutes each side until singed and puffy.

beef & barley brö

Serves **6**
Preparation time **20 minutes**
Cooking time **2 hours**

2 tablespoons **butter**
8 oz **braising beef**, fat
   trimmed away and meat cut
   into small cubes
1 large **onion**, finely chopped
1 cup diced **rutabaga**
1 cup diced **carrot**
½ cup **pearl barley**
8 cups **beef stock** (see
   page 12)
2 teaspoons **powdered
   English mustard** (optional)
salt and **pepper**
chopped **parsley**, to garnish

Heat the butter in a large saucepan, add the beef and onion, and fry for 5 minutes, stirring, until the beef is browned and the onion just beginning to brown.

Stir in the diced vegetables, pearl barley, stock, and mustard, if using. Season with salt and pepper and bring to a boil. Cover and simmer for 1¾ hours, stirring occasionally, until the meat and vegetables are very tender. Taste and adjust the seasoning if needed. Ladle the soup into bowls and sprinkle with a little chopped parsley. Serve with warm potato bannocks or farls.

For lamb & barley hotchpot, substitute the beef with 8 oz diced lamb loin and fry with the onion as above. Add the sliced white part of 1 leek, 1 cup each of diced rutabaga, carrot, and potato, then mix in ¼ cup pearl barley, 8 cups lamb stock, 2–3 sprigs of rosemary, and salt and pepper. Bring to a boil then cover and simmer for 1¾ hours. Discard the rosemary, add the remaining thinly sliced green leek, and cook for 10 minutes. Ladle into bowls and sprinkle with a little extra chopped rosemary to serve.

cock-a-leekie soup

Serves **6**
Preparation time **30 minutes**
Cooking time **2 hours**

1 tablespoon **sunflower oil**
2 **chicken thigh** and **leg joints**, about 12 oz
1 lb **leeks**, thinly sliced, white and green parts kept separate
3 **bacon slices**, diced
2½ quarts **chicken stock** (see page 10)
⅓ cup **pitted prunes**, quartered
1 **bay leaf**
1 large **thyme sprig**
¼ cup **long-grain rice**
salt and **pepper**

Heat the oil in a large saucepan, add the chicken joints, and fry on one side until golden. Turn them over and add the white sliced leeks and bacon. Fry until the chicken is golden all over and the leeks and bacon just beginning to brown.

Pour in the stock, then add the prunes, bay leaf, and thyme, season with salt and pepper and bring to a boil. Cover and simmer for 1½ hours, stirring occasionally until the chicken is falling off the bones.

Lift the chicken, bay leaf, and thyme sprigs out of the soup with a slotted spoon and put onto a plate. Remove the skin and bones from the chicken then cut the meat into pieces. Return the chicken to the pan, adding the rice and green leek slices. Simmer for 10 minutes until the rice and leeks are tender.

Taste and adjust the seasoning if needed. Ladle the soup into bowls and serve with warm, crusty bread.

For cream of chicken soup, omit the prunes and rice and use only 8 cups stock. Add 1 cup diced potato then bring to a boil and simmer for 1½ hours. Discard the herbs and puree the soup in batches in a blender or food processor. Stir in ⅔ cup milk and ⅔ cup heavy cream. Reheat and serve with croutons (see page 15).

spring vegetable broth

Serves **4**

Preparation time **15 minutes**

Cooking time **30–35 minutes**

2 teaspoons **olive oil**

2 **celery sticks** with their leaves, chopped

2 **leeks**, chopped

1 **carrot**, finely diced

¼ cup **pearl barley**

5 cups **vegetable stock** (see page 13)

1 teaspoon **English mustard**

1½ cups **snow peas**, sliced diagonally (optional)

salt and **pepper**

Heat the oil in a saucepan and add the celery, leeks, and carrot. Cook over a medium heat for 5 minutes.

Stir in the pearl barley, stock, and mustard, season to taste and simmer for 20–25 minutes. Add the snow peas, if desired, and simmer for 5 minutes.

Ladle into warmed soup bowls and serve piping hot.

For winter vegetable broth, make up the soup as above using just 1 chopped leek and adding ½ cup finely diced rutabaga. Simmer for 20 minutes then add 1 cup finely shredded green cabbage instead of the snow peas. Simmer for 10 minutes then ladle into bowls and top with diced crispy broiled bacon.

onion, tomato, & chickpea soup

Serves **6**

Preparation time **15 minutes**

Cooking time **1 hour 10 minutes**

2 tablespoons **olive oil**

2 **red onions**, roughly chopped

2 **garlic cloves**, finely chopped

2 teaspoons **brown sugar**

1¼ lb **tomatoes**, skinned if desired, roughly chopped

2 teaspoons **harissa paste**

3 teaspoons **tomato paste**

13 oz can **chickpeas**, drained

3¾ cups **vegetable** or **chicken stock** (see pages 13 and 10)

salt and **pepper**

Heat the oil in a large saucepan, add the onions, and fry over a low heat for 10 minutes, stirring occasionally until just beginning to brown around the edges. Stir in the garlic and sugar and cook for 10 more minutes, stirring more frequently as the onions begin to caramelize.

Stir in the tomatoes and harissa paste and fry for 5 minutes. Mix in the tomato paste, chickpeas, stock, and salt and pepper and bring to a boil. Cover and simmer for 45 minutes until the tomatoes and onion are very soft. Taste and adjust the seasoning if needed.

Ladle into bowls and serve with warm tomato ciabatta.

For chilied red onion & bean soup, make up the soup as above but omit the harissa and add 1 teaspoon of smoked paprika and 1 split dried red chili when frying the tomatoes, then swap the chickpeas for the same size can of red kidney beans. Serve with garlic bread.

veg soup with bacon dumplings

Serves **6**
Preparation time **30 minutes**
Cooking time **1¼–1½ hours**

¼ cup **butter**
1 **onion**, finely chopped
1 **leek**, diced, white and green
   parts kept separate
10 oz **rutabaga**, diced
10 oz **parsnip**, diced
10 oz **carrot**, diced
2 **celery sticks**, diced
3–4 **sage** stems
2½ quarts **chicken stock** (see
   page 10)
salt and **pepper**

Dumplings
1 cup **self-rising flour**
½ teaspoon **powdered
   English mustard**
2 teaspoons finely chopped
   sage
½ cup **vegetable suet**
2 **bacon slices**, finely
   chopped
4 tablespoons **water**

Heat the butter in a large saucepan, add the onion and white diced leeks, and fry for 5 minutes until just beginning to soften. Add the other diced vegetables and sage, toss in the butter, then cover and fry for 10 minutes, stirring occasionally.

Pour on the stock, season with salt and pepper, and bring to a boil. Cover and simmer for 45 minutes, stirring occasionally until the vegetables are tender. Remove the sage then taste and adjust the seasoning if needed.

Make the dumplings by mixing the flour, powdered mustard, sage, suet, and bacon in a bowl with a little salt and pepper. Gradually stir in the water and mix first with a spoon, then squeeze together with your hands to make a smooth dough. Cut into 18 slices and roll each slice into a into small ball.

Stir the remaining green diced leek into the soup. Add the dumplings to the simmering soup, re-cover the pan, and cook for 10 minutes until the dumplings are light and fluffy. Ladle into bowls and serve immediately.

For creamy winter vegetable soup, omit the dumplings and reduce the amount of stock to 6 cups. Simmer for 45 minutes then puree in batches in a blender or food processor. Pour back into the saucepan, stir in 1¼ cups milk and reheat. Ladle into bowls, swirl 2 tablespoons of heavy cream into each portion and garnish with a little chopped sage and some crispy diced bacon.

christmas special

Serves **6**

Preparation **25 minutes**

Cooking time **about 1 hour**

2 tablespoons **butter**

1 **onion**, roughly chopped

2 **bacon slices**, diced

2 cups diced **potato**

4 cups **chicken** or **turkey stock** (see page 10)

4 oz **vacuum-packed peeled chestnuts**

large pinch of **grated nutmeg**

8 oz **Brussels sprouts**, sliced

salt and **pepper**

4 **bacon slices**, broiled and diced, to garnish

Heat the butter in a saucepan, add the onion, and fry gently for 5 minutes until softened. Add the bacon and potato, toss in the butter, then cover and fry for 5 minutes until just beginning to brown.

Pour on the stock, crumble in the chestnuts, then add the nutmeg and salt and pepper. Bring to a boil, then cover and simmer for 30 minutes. Add the sliced sprouts and mix into the stock, then cover and simmer for 5 minutes until they are tender but still bright green.

Allow the soup to cool slightly, reserve a few sprout slices for the garnish, then puree it in batches in a blender or food processor until green specks can still be seen. Pour back into the saucepan and reheat. Taste and adjust the seasoning if needed. Garnish with the remaining Brussels sprouts and bacon.

For chestnut & mushroom soup, omit the Brussels sprouts and add 8 oz sliced cup mushrooms after frying the potatoes and bacon and cook for 2–3 minutes, stirring frequently. Add the stock, chestnuts, nutmeg, and salt and pepper, then bring to a boil and cook for 30 minutes. Puree and reheat the soup and serve garnished with cream, bacon, and chestnuts as above.

harira

Serves **8–10**

Preparation time **about 25 minutes, plus soaking**

Cooking time **about 3 hours**

1 ½ cups **chickpeas**, soaked in cold water overnight

2 **chicken breasts**, halved

5 cups **chicken stock** (see page 10)

5 cups **water**

2 x 13 oz cans **chopped tomatoes**

¼ teaspoon crumbled **saffron threads** (optional)

2 **onions**, chopped

½ cup **long-grain rice**

¼ cup **green lentils**

2 tablespoons finely chopped **cilantro**

2 tablespoons finely chopped **parsley**

salt and **pepper**

To garnish
plain yogurt
cilantro sprigs

Drain the chickpeas, rinse under cold running water and drain again. Place them in a saucepan, cover with 2 inches of water, and bring to a boil. Boil rapidly for 10 minutes, then lower the heat and simmer, partially covered, until tender, adding more water as necessary. This will take anything up to 1¾ hours. Drain the chickpeas and set aside.

Place the chicken breasts, stock, and water in a second saucepan. Bring to a boil, lower the heat, cover, and simmer for 10–15 minutes or until the chicken is just cooked. Remove the chicken from the stock, place it on a board and shred it, discarding the skin.

Set the shredded chicken aside. Add the chickpeas, tomatoes, saffron (if using), onions, rice, and lentils to the stock remaining in the pan. Cover the pan and simmer for 30–35 minutes or until the rice and lentils are tender.

Add the shredded chicken, cilantro, and parsley just before serving. Heat the soup for an additional 5 minutes without letting it boil. Season to taste and serve the soup, garnished with drizzles of plain yogurt and cilantro sprigs.

For budget harira, make up the soup as above omitting the chicken breasts and saffron, adding ½ teaspoon ground turmeric and ½ teaspoon ground cinnamon instead.

thai squash & cilantro soup

Serves **6**

Preparation time **25 minutes**

Cooking time **51 minutes**

1 tablespoon **sunflower oil**

1 **onion**, roughly chopped

3 teaspoons **ready-made red Thai curry paste**

1–2 **garlic cloves**, finely chopped

1 inch piece of **fresh ginger root**, peeled and finely chopped

1 **butternut squash**, about 1½ lb, halved, seeded, peeled, and diced

1¾ cups **full-fat coconut milk**

3 cups **vegetable** or **chicken stock** (see pages 13 and 10)

2 teaspoons **Thai fish sauce**

pepper

small bunch of **cilantro**

Heat the oil in a saucepan, add the onion, and fry gently for 5 minutes until softened. Stir in the curry paste, garlic, and ginger and cook for 1 minute. Then mix in the squash, coconut milk, stock, and fish sauce. Add a little pepper (don't add salt as the fish sauce is so salty) then bring to a boil.

Cover the pan and simmer for 45 minutes, stirring occasionally, until the squash is soft. Allow to cool slightly. Reserve a few sprigs of cilantro for garnish then tear the remainder into pieces and add to the soup. Puree the soup in batches in a blender or food processor until smooth. Pour back into the saucepan and reheat, tearing in the reserved cilantro sprigs. Ladle into bowls and serve.

For gingered squash soup, omit the Thai curry paste, coconut milk, fish sauce, and cilantro. Fry the onion as above then mix in the garlic and a 1½ inch piece of peeled and finely chopped fresh ginger root. Add the squash as above, 3¾ cups of stock and a little salt and pepper, then bring to a boil. Cover and simmer for 45 minutes then puree and mix with 1¼ cups milk. Reheat and serve with croutons (see page 15).

red pepper soup & pesto stifato

Serves **6**
Preparation time **30 minutes**
Cooking time **about 1 hour**

4 **red bell peppers**, halved,
    cored, and seeded
3 tablespoons **olive oil**
1 large **onion**, roughly
    chopped
2–3 **garlic cloves**, finely
    chopped
13 oz can **chopped tomatoes**
3¾ cups **vegetable** or
    chicken stock (see pages
    13 and 10)
2 tablespoons **balsamic
    vinegar**
salt and **pepper**

To garnish
olive oil
handful of **basil leaves**
black pepper

Pesto stifato
2 **stifato sticks**, or long thin
    bread rolls
2 tablespoons **pesto**
½ cup grated **Parmesan
    cheese**

Arrange the peppers skin-side up in a foil-lined broiler pan, brush with 2 tablespoons of the oil, then broil for about 10 minutes until the skins are blackened and the peppers softened. Wrap the foil around the peppers, then allow them to cool for 10 minutes.

Meanwhile, heat the remaining oil in a saucepan, add the onion, and fry gently for 5 minutes until softened and just beginning to brown. Mix in the garlic and cook for 1 minute, then mix in the tomatoes, stock, vinegar, and salt and pepper.

Peel the blackened skins off the peppers then roughly chop the peppers. Add to the saucepan, then bring to a boil, cover, and simmer for 30 minutes. Allow to cool slightly, then puree in batches in a blender or food processor until smooth.

Return the soup to the pan, reheat, then taste and adjust the seasoning if needed. Cut the stifato sticks or bread rolls into long strips, then lightly toast on both sides. Spread with the pesto then sprinkle with the cheese and broil until just melting. Ladle the soup into bowls and drizzle with some olive oil, a few basil leaves, and some black pepper.

For roasted red pepper & cannellini bean soup,
broil the peppers as above. Skin and finely chop the peppers, then add to the fried onion, tomato, and stock mixture. Omit the balsamic vinegar and add 3 large pinches of saffron threads and a drained 13½ oz can cannellini beans. Season then cover and simmer for 30 minutes. Do not puree, but serve the soup chunky with garlic bread.

beef & noodle broth

Serves **2**
Preparation time **15 minutes**
Cooking time **15 minutes**

10 oz **sirloin steak**
1 inch piece of **fresh ginger root**, grated
2 teaspoons **soy sauce**
2 oz **vermicelli rice noodles**
2½ cups **beef** or **chicken stock** (see pages 12 and 10)
1 **red chili**, seeded and finely chopped
1 **garlic clove**, thinly sliced
2 teaspoons **superfine sugar**
2 teaspoons **vegetable oil**
3 oz **sugar snap peas**, halved lengthwise
small handful of **Thai basil**, torn into pieces

Trim any fat from the beef. Mix the ginger with 1 teaspoon of the soy sauce and smooth over both sides of the beef. Cook the noodles according to the directions on the package. Drain and rinse thoroughly in cold water.

Bring the stock to a gentle simmer with the chili, garlic, and sugar. Cover and cook gently for 5 minutes.

Heat the oil in a small, heavy skillet and fry the beef for 2 minutes on each side. Transfer the meat to a board, cut it in half lengthwise and then cut it across into thin strips.

Add the noodles, sugar snap peas, basil, and remaining soy sauce to the soup and heat gently for 1 minute. Stir in the beef and serve immediately.

For minted chicken broth, replace the steak with the same weight of boneless, skinless chicken breasts and use chicken stock instead of beef. Make the soup as above, but fry the chicken for 5–6 minutes on each side until thoroughly cooked. Garnish the soup with a small bunch of torn mint.

squash, kale, & mixed bean soup

Serves **6**
Preparation time **15 minutes**
Cooking time **45 minutes**

1 tablespoon **olive oil**
1 **onion**, finely chopped
2 **garlic cloves**, finely
  chopped
1 teaspoon **smoked paprika**
1 lb **butternut squash**, sliced,
  seeded, peeled, and diced
2 small **carrots**, diced
1 lb **tomatoes**, skinned
  optional, roughly chopped
13½ oz can **mixed beans**,
  drained
3¾ cups **vegetable** or
  chicken stock (see pages
  13 and 10)
⅔ cup **full-fat sour cream**
1 cup **kale**, torn into bite-size
  pieces
salt and **pepper**

Heat the oil in a saucepan, add the onion, and fry gently for 5 minutes. Stir in the garlic and smoked paprika and cook briefly, then add the squash, carrots, tomatoes, and drained beans.

Pour on the stock, season with salt and pepper, and bring to a boil, stirring. Cover and simmer for 25 minutes until the vegetables are tender.

Stir the sour cream into the soup, then add the kale, pressing it just beneath the surface of the stock. Cover and cook for 5 minutes until the kale has just wilted. Ladle into bowls and serve with warm garlic bread.

For cheesy squash, pepper, & mixed bean soup, fry the onion in oil as above, add the garlic, smoked paprika, squash, tomatoes, and beans, adding a seeded and diced red bell pepper instead of the carrot. Pour on the stock, then add 2½ oz Parmesan rinds and season. Cover and simmer for 25 minutes. Stir in the sour cream but omit the kale. Discard the Parmesan rinds, ladle the soup into bowls, and top with freshly grated Parmesan.

butternut squash & rosemary soup

Serves **4**
Preparation time **15 minutes**
Cooking time **1¼ hours**

1 **butternut squash**
2 tablespoons **olive oil**
a few **rosemary sprigs**, plus
    extra to garnish
¾ cup **red lentils**, washed
1 **onion**, finely chopped
3¾ cups **vegetable stock**
    (see page 13)
salt and **pepper**

Cut the squash in half and use a spoon to scoop out the seeds and fibrous flesh. Peel and cut the squash into small chunks and place in a roasting pan. Sprinkle with the oil and rosemary, and season well with salt and pepper. Roast in a preheated oven, 400°F, for 45 minutes.

Meanwhile, place the lentils in a saucepan, cover with water, bring to a boil and boil rapidly for 10 minutes. Strain, then return the lentils to a clean saucepan with the onion and stock and simmer for 5 minutes. Season to taste.

Remove the squash from the oven, mash the flesh with a fork and add to the soup. Simmer for 25 minutes and then ladle into bowls. Garnish with more rosemary before serving.

For Indian spiced butternut squash soup, roast the squash and cook the lentils as above then drain. Heat 1 tablespoon sunflower oil in a saucepan, add 1 chopped onion and fry for 5 minutes until softened. Stir in 2 teaspoons mild curry paste and a 1½ inch piece of fresh ginger root, finely chopped. Add the drained lentils and stock and simmer for 5 minutes. Mash the squash as above and stir into the soup. Garnish with torn cilantro leaves.

honey-roasted parsnip soup

Serves **6**
Preparation time **20 minutes**
Cooking time **50–55 minutes**

1½ lb **parsnips**, cut into
  wedges
2 **onions**, cut into wedges
2 tablespoons **olive oil**
2 tablespoons **honey**
1 teaspoon **ground turmeric**
½ teaspoon **dried red pepper
  flakes**
3 **garlic cloves**, thickly sliced
5 cups **vegetable** or **chicken
  stock** (see pages 13 and
  10)
2 tablespoons **sherry** or **cider
  vinegar**
⅔ cup **heavy cream**
2 inch piece of **fresh ginger
  root**, peeled and grated
salt and **pepper**
a little **turmeric**, to garnish

Arrange the parsnips and onions in a large roasting
pan in a single layer, then drizzle with the oil and honey.
Sprinkle with the turmeric, pepper flakes, and garlic.

Roast in a preheated oven, 375°F, for 45–50 minutes,
turning once until a deep golden brown with sticky,
caramelized edges.

Transfer the roasting pan to the stove top, add the
stock, vinegar, and salt and pepper and bring to a boil,
scraping up the juices from the base of the pan.
Simmer for 5 minutes.

Allow the soup to cool slightly, then puree in batches
in a blender or food processor until smooth. Pour into
a saucepan and reheat. Taste and adjust the seasoning
and top up with a little extra stock, if needed. Mix the
cream, ginger, and a little pepper together. Ladle the
soup into bowls and drizzle the ginger cream over the
top, then garnish with a little turmeric, if desired. Serve
with croutons (see page 15).

For honey-roasted sweet potato soup, replace the
parsnips with 1½ lb sweet potato, cut into wedges,
sprinkle with 1 teaspoon roughly crushed cumin seeds
in addition to the turmeric and pepper, and roast and
finish as above. Serve ladled into soup bowls topped
with spoonfuls of plain yogurt and a teaspoon of
mango chutney drizzled over each bowl.

split pea & parsnip soup

Serves **6**
Preparation time **20 minutes**
Cooking time **1¼ hours**

1¼ cups **yellow split peas**,
   soaked overnight in cold
   water
10 oz **parsnips**, cut into
   chunks
1 **onion**, roughly chopped
6 cups **chicken** or **vegetable
   stock** (see pages 10
   and 13)
salt and **pepper**

Cilantro butter
1 teaspoon **cumin seeds**,
   roughly crushed
1 teaspoon **cilantro seeds**,
   roughly crushed
2 **garlic cloves**, finely
   chopped
⅓ cup **butter**
small bunch of **cilantro**

Drain the soaked split peas and put them into a
saucepan with the parsnips, onion, and stock. Bring
to a boil and boil for 10 minutes. Reduce the heat,
cover, and simmer for 1 hour or until the split peas
are soft.

Meanwhile, make the butter by dry-frying the cumin
and cilantro seeds and garlic in a small saucepan until
lightly toasted. Mix into the butter with the cilantro
leaves and a little salt and pepper. Shape into a
sausage shape on plastic wrap or foil, wrap up, and
chill until needed.

Roughly mash the soup or puree in batches in a
blender or food processor, if preferred. Reheat and stir
in half the cilantro butter until melted. Add a little extra
stock if needed then season to taste. Ladle into bowls
and top each bowl with a slice of the cilantro butter.
Serve with toasted pita breads.

For split pea & carrot soup with chili butter, make
up the soup with 2 cups diced carrots in place of the
parsnips. Puree and reheat as above. Make a chili
butter by mixing ⅓ cup butter with the grated zest and
juice of 1 lime, 2 chopped scallions, and ½–1 large
mild and finely chopped red chili to taste.

beer broth with mini meatballs

Serves **6**
Preparation time **25 minutes**
Cooking time **about 1¼ hours**

2 tablespoons **butter**
1 **onion**, chopped
2 cups diced **potato**
1 cup diced **rutabaga** or
    parsnip
1 **carrot**, diced
2 **tomatoes**, skinned if
    desired, roughly chopped
½ **lemon**, sliced
3¾ cups **beef stock** (see
    page 12)
1 can **beer**
¼ teaspoon **ground
    cinnamon**
¼ teaspoon **grated nutmeg**
1 cup finely shredded **green
    cabbage**
salt and **pepper**

Meatballs
8 oz **extra-lean ground beef**
3 tablespoons **long-grain rice**
3 tablespoons chopped
    parsley, plus extra to garnish
¼ teaspoon **grated nutmeg**

Heat the butter in a large saucepan, add the onion, and fry gently for 5 minutes until just turning golden around the edges. Stir in the diced root vegetables, the tomatoes, and lemon.

Pour in the stock and beer, then add the spices and season well with salt and pepper. Bring to a boil, stirring, then cover and simmer for 45 minutes.

Meanwhile, mix all the meatball ingredients together. Divide into 18 and shape into small balls with wetted hands. Chill until needed.

Add the meatballs to the soup, bring the soup back to a boil then cover and simmer for 10 minutes. Add the cabbage and cook for 10 minutes until the cabbage is tender and the meatballs cooked all the way through. Taste and adjust the seasoning. Ladle into shallow bowls and sprinkle with a little chopped parsley if desired.

For beer broth with suet dumplings, gently fry 1 lb thinly sliced onions in the butter for 20 minutes until very soft. Sprinkle with 2 teaspoons brown sugar and fry for 10 minutes, stirring until caramelized. Add the lemon slices, stock, beer, and spices, omitting the root vegetables and tomatoes. Simmer for 20 minutes. Mix 1 cup self-rising flour with ½ cup vegetable suet, 2 tablespoons chopped parsley, and salt and pepper. Stir in 4 tablespoons water, then shape into small balls. Add to the simmering soup, cook for 10 minutes then ladle into bowls and serve.

cheesy butternut squash soup

Serves **6**
Preparation time **25 minutes**
Cooking time **about 1 hour**

2 tablespoons **olive oil**
1 **onion**, roughly chopped
1 **butternut squash**, about
   1½ lb, halved, seeded,
   peeled, and cut into chunks
1–2 **garlic cloves**, finely
   chopped
2 large **sage sprigs**
4 cups **chicken** or **vegetable**
   stock (see pages 10
   and 13)
2½ oz **Parmesan rinds**
salt and **pepper**

To finish
oil for deep-frying
small bunch of **sage**
grated **Parmesan cheese**

Heat the oil in a saucepan, add the onion, and fry for 5 minutes until softened and just beginning to turn golden. Add the squash, garlic, and sage and fry for 5 minutes, stirring.

Pour in the stock and add the Parmesan rinds and salt and pepper. Bring to a boil then cover and simmer for 45 minutes until the squash is tender.

Scoop out and discard the sage and Parmesan rinds. Allow the soup to cool slightly, then puree in batches in a blender or food processor until smooth. Return to the saucepan and reheat. Add a little extra stock if needed then taste and adjust the seasoning.

Fill a small saucepan halfway with oil and heat until a cube of day-old bread sizzles the minute it is added. Then tear the sage leaves from the stems and add to the oil, frying for a minute or two until crisp. Lift out with a slotted spoon and put onto paper towels.

Ladle the soup into bowls, top with some of the crispy sage and a sprinkling of grated Parmesan, serving the remaining leaves and extra Parmesan in small bowls for diners to add their own as desired.

For Halloween pumpkin soup, fry the onion as above. Quarter a 3 lb pumpkin, scoop out the seeds, peel, and cut into cubes and add to the onion and fry for 5 minutes. Stir in 1 teaspoon ground cumin, 1 teaspoon ground coriander, and 1 teaspoon ground ginger instead of the garlic and sage, then pour in the stock. Cover and simmer for 30 minutes, then puree and reheat the soup as above. Serve with moon- and star-shaped croutons cut with cookie cutters.

beery oxtail & lima bean soup

Serves **6**
Preparation time **25 minutes**
Cooking time **4¼ hours**

1 tablespoon **sunflower oil**
1 lb **oxtail pieces**, string
   removed
1 **onion**, finely chopped
2 **carrots**, diced
2 **celery sticks**, diced
2 cups diced **potatoes**
small bunch of **mixed herbs**
8 cups **beef stock** (see
   page 12)
1¾ cups **English beer**
2 teaspoons **English mustard**
2 tablespoons **Worcestershire
   sauce**
1 tablespoon **tomato paste**
13½ oz can **lima beans**,
   drained
salt and **pepper**
chopped **parsley**, to garnish

Heat the oil in a large saucepan, add the oxtail pieces, and fry until browned on one side. Turn the oxtail pieces over and add the onion, stirring until browned on all sides. Stir in the carrots, celery, potatoes, and herbs and cook for 2–3 more minutes.

Pour in the stock and ale, then add the mustard, Worcestershire sauce, tomato paste, and lima beans. Season well with salt and pepper and bring to a boil, stirring. Half cover the pan and simmer gently for 4 hours.

Lift the oxtail and herbs out of the pan with a slotted spoon. Discard the herbs and cut the meat off the oxtail bones, discarding any fat. Return the meat to the pan, reheat, then taste and adjust the seasoning if needed. Ladle into bowls, sprinkle with chopped parsley, and serve with crusty bread.

For chilied oxtail & red bean soup, omit the bunch of mixed herbs and instead stir 2 finely chopped garlic cloves, 2 bay leaves, 1 teaspoon hot chili powder, 1 teaspoon crushed cumin seeds, and 1 teaspoon crushed coriander seeds into the vegetables. Then add the beef stock, a 13 oz can chopped tomatoes, 1 tablespoon tomato paste, and a drained 13½ oz can of red kidney beans. Bring to a boil, simmer, and finish as above.

kale soup with garlic croutons

Serves **8–10**

Preparation time **20–25 minutes**

Cooking time **50 minutes**

¼ cup **butter** or **margarine**

1 **onion**, chopped

2 **carrots**, sliced

1 lb **kale**, thick stems removed and discarded

5 cups **water**

2½ cups **vegetable stock** (see page 13)

1 tablespoon **lemon juice**

10 oz **potatoes**, peeled and sliced

pinch of **grated nutmeg**

salt and **pepper**

2 **kale leaves**, thinly shredded, to garnish

Garlic croutons

6–8 slices of **white** or **brown bread**, crusts removed

6–8 tablespoons **olive oil**

3 **garlic cloves**, sliced

Melt the butter or margarine in a large saucepan, add the onion, and fry for 5 minutes until softened and just beginning to turn golden. Add the carrots and kale in batches, stirring all the time, and cook for 2 minutes.

Add the water, stock, lemon juice, potatoes, and nutmeg, with salt and pepper to taste. Bring to a boil, stirring from time to time. Lower the heat, cover, and simmer for 35 minutes or until all the vegetables are soft. Puree the mixture in batches in a blender or food processor, adding extra water if it is too thick.

Prepare the croutons by cutting the bread into ½ inch cubes. Heat the oil in a large skillet, add the garlic, and cook over a moderate heat for 1 minute. Add the bread squares and fry, turning frequently, until evenly golden brown. Transfer the croutons to paper towels with a slotted spoon to drain. Discard the garlic, then add the thinly shredded kale to the pan and fry, stirring constantly until crispy.

Taste the soup and adjust the seasoning if needed and reheat without boiling. Serve in heated soup plates with the garlic croutons and crispy kale.

For spiced kale soup, fry the onion as above, add the carrots and kale in batches then stir in 1 teaspoon smoked paprika and 2 chopped garlic cloves and cook for 2 minutes. Continue as above, adding ¼ teaspoon dried red pepper flakes to the oil when frying the croutons.

something
special

cheat's bouillabaisse

Serves **6**
Preparation time **15 minutes**
Cooking time **30 minutes**

2 tablespoons **olive oil**
1 large **onion**, finely chopped
1 **leek**, thinly sliced
2 large pinches of **saffron threads**
2 **garlic cloves**, finely chopped
1 lb **plum tomatoes**, skinned, roughly chopped
⅔ cup **dry white wine**
2½ cups **fish stock** (see page 13)
2–3 **thyme stems**, leaves torn from stems
1 lb firm **white fish (angler fish, hake, haddock, or cod)**, skinned and cubed
13 oz **frozen mixed seafood**, defrosted, rinsed with cold water, and drained
salt and **pepper**
½ small **French loaf**, sliced and toasted

Heat the oil in a large saucepan, add the onion and leek, and fry gently for 5 minutes, stirring until softened. Meanwhile soak the saffron in 1 tablespoon boiling water.

Add the garlic and tomatoes to the pan and fry for 2–3 minutes then mix in the soaked saffron, wine, stock, thyme, and some salt and pepper. Cover and simmer for 10 minutes.

Add the white fish, re-cover and simmer gently for 3 minutes. Add the mixed seafood, re-cover, and simmer gently for 5 more minutes until all the fish is just cooked. Ladle into bowls and serve with toasted bread topped with spoonfuls of rouille (see below).

For homemade rouille, to serve as an accompaniment, drain 3 roasted red peppers from a jar, put into a blender or food processor with 2–3 garlic cloves, 1 teaspoon finely chopped red chili (from a jar), 1 slice white bread torn into pieces, a large pinch of saffron threads soaked in 1 tablespoon boiling water, and 3 tablespoons olive oil. Blend until smooth and spoon into a small bowl.

pumpkin, orange, & star anise soup

Serves **6**
Preparation time **25 minutes**
Cooking time **50 minutes**

2 tablespoons **butter**
1 **onion**, roughly chopped
1 small **pumpkin**, about 3 lb,
   quartered, seeded, peeled,
   then diced
2 small **oranges**, zest
   removed with a zester, juice
   squeezed
4 cups **vegetable** or **chicken
   stock** (see pages 13
   and 10)
3 whole **star anise** or similar
   amount in pieces, plus extra
   to garnish
salt and **pepper**
crushed **black peppercorns**,
   to garnish (optional)

Heat the butter in a large saucepan, add the onion, and fry gently for 5 minutes until softened. Add the pumpkin, toss in the butter, and fry for 5 minutes, stirring.

Mix in the orange zest and juice, the stock, and star anise. Season with salt and pepper and bring to a boil. Cover and simmer for 30 minutes, stirring occasionally until the pumpkin is soft. Scoop out the star anise and reserve.

Allow the soup to cool slightly, then puree in batches in a blender or food processor until smooth. Pour back into the saucepan and reheat. Taste and adjust the seasoning if needed.

Ladle the soup into bowls and garnish each bowl with a whole star anise and a sprinkling of black pepper, or a slice of spiced orange and chili butter. Serve with sesame bread rolls.

For homemade spiced orange & chili butter,

to serve as an accompaniment, beat ⅓ cup butter with the grated zest of 1 orange, a large mild, seeded and finely chopped red chili, a pinch of ground turmeric, and a pinch of ground cloves. Shape into a sausage then wrap in plastic wrap. Chill then unwrap, slice, and add to soup just before serving.

gingered cauliflower soup

Serves **6**
Preparation time **25 minutes**
Cooking time **25 minutes**

1 tablespoon **sunflower oil**
2 tablespoons **butter**
1 **onion**, roughly chopped
1 **cauliflower**, cut into florets,
   woody core discarded,
   about 2 cups when prepared
1½ inch piece of **fresh ginger
   root**, peeled and finely
   chopped
3¾ cups **vegetable** or
   chicken stock (see pages
   13 and 10)
1¼ cups **milk**
⅔ cup **heavy cream**
salt and **pepper**

Soy-glazed seeds

1 tablespoon **sunflower oil**
2 tablespoons **sesame seeds**
2 tablespoons **sunflower
   seeds**
2 tablespoons **pumpkin
   seeds**
1 tablespoon **soy sauce**

Heat the oil and butter in a saucepan, add the onion, and fry for 5 minutes until softened but not browned. Stir in the cauliflower florets and ginger, then the stock. Season with salt and pepper and bring to a boil. Cover and simmer for 15 minutes until the cauliflower is just tender.

Meanwhile, make the glazed seeds by heating the oil in a skillet, add the seeds, and cook for 2–3 minutes, stirring until lightly browned. Add the soy sauce, then quickly cover the pan with a lid until the seeds have stopped popping. Set aside until ready to serve.

Puree the cooked soup in batches in a blender or food processor, then pour back into the saucepan and stir in the milk and half the cream. Bring just to a boil, then taste and adjust the seasoning if needed.

Ladle the soup into shallow bowls, drizzle over the rest of the cream, and sprinkle with some of the glazed seeds, serving the remaining seeds in a small bowl for additional sprinkling.

For creamy cauliflower & cashew soup, heat the oil and butter as above then add the chopped onion and ⅓ cup cashew nuts and fry until the onions are softened and the nuts very lightly browned. Mix in the cauliflower florets and stock as above, then season with salt, pepper, and a little grated nutmeg. Simmer for 15 minutes. Puree and finish with milk and cream as above, ladle into bowls, and garnish with ⅓ cup cashew nuts fried in 1 tablespoon butter until pale golden, then cooked for 1–2 minutes more with 1 tablespoon honey until golden and caramelized.

spinach bouillabaisse

Serves **6**

Preparation time **15 minutes**

Cooking time **about 30 minutes**

2 tablespoons **olive oil**

1 **onion**, finely chopped

1 **fennel bulb**, diced

3 cups diced **potatoes**

4 **garlic cloves**, finely chopped

3 large pinches of **saffron threads**

7 cups **vegetable** or **chicken stock** (see pages 13 and 10)

⅔ cup **dry white wine**

2½ cups **baby leaf spinach**, rinsed and drained

6 **eggs**

salt and **pepper**

Heat the oil in a large saucepan (or shallow sauté pan if possible) then add the onion and fry for 5 minutes until just beginning to soften. Add the fennel, reserving any green fronds for later, the potato, and the garlic and fry for 5 more minutes, stirring.

Mix in the saffron, stock, and white wine, then season with salt and pepper and bring to a boil. Cover and simmer for 15 minutes, stirring occasionally or until the potatoes are tender.

Add the spinach, tearing the larger leaves into pieces, and cook for 2–3 minutes until just beginning to wilt. Taste and adjust the seasoning if needed. Scoop out most of the vegetables with a slotted spoon and divide between warmed shallow serving bowls. Add the eggs one at a time to the remaining hot stock, leaving a little space between them and simmer gently for 3–4 minutes until the whites are just set and the yolks are cooked to your preference.

Lift the poached eggs out of the soup carefully with a slotted spoon and place on top of the vegetables in the soup bowls. Ladle the stock around the eggs, top with any reserved and snipped green fennel fronds, and sprinkle with black pepper. Serve with toasted olive ciabatta bread.

For creamy spinach & fennel soup, make the soup as above, with 5 cups stock and ⅔ cup white wine. Puree the soup in batches in a blender or food processor when the spinach has just wilted. Reheat, omit the eggs, and serve topped with spoonfuls of sour cream and some fennel or dill fronds.

apple & celery soup

Serves **6**
Preparation time **25 minutes**
Cooking time **about 40 minutes**

2 tablespoons **butter**
1 **onion**, roughly chopped
1 **baking potato**, about 8 oz, diced
1 **cooking apple**, about 8 oz, quartered, cored, peeled, then diced
1 **head of celery**, base trimmed
3 cups **chicken** or **vegetable stock** (see pages 10 and 13)
1¼ cups **milk**
salt and **pepper**

Stilton & walnut cream
2 oz **Stilton cheese**, rind removed, cheese diced
¼ cup **walnut pieces**, chopped
6 tablespoons **full-fat sour cream**
2 tablespoons chopped **chives** or tops of 2 **scallions**, chopped

Heat the butter in a saucepan, add the onion, and fry for 5 minutes until just beginning to soften. Stir in the potato and apple, cover, and fry gently for 10 minutes, stirring occasionally.

Reserve the tiny celery leaves from the center of the celery for garnish and keep in a bowl of cold water until needed. Thickly slice the rest of the stems and add with the larger leaves to the onion and stir-fry for 2–3 minutes. Pour on the stock then season with salt and pepper and bring to a boil. Cover and simmer for 15 minutes until the celery is soft but still a pale green.

Puree the soup in batches in a blender or food processor until smooth. Return to the saucepan, stir in the milk and then reheat. Taste and adjust the seasoning if needed.

Stir half the diced cheese and half the walnuts into the sour cream, then mix in the chives or scallion and a little salt and pepper. Ladle the soup into shallow bowls, then spoon the sour cream mixture into the center. Sprinkle with the remaining cheese and nuts and add a little black pepper.

For apple & parsnip soup, omit the potato and celery adding 1¼ lb diced parsnips when frying the apple. Stir in 1½ teaspoons crushed cumin seeds and ½ teaspoon turmeric, then mix in 3¾ cups of vegetable or chicken stock and season. Bring to a boil then cover and simmer for 45 minutes. Puree and reheat with the milk. Make the Stilton and sour cream mixture as above, adding ½ teaspoon finely chopped red chili instead of the walnuts.

asian mussel soup

Serves **4**

Preparation time **25 minutes**

Cooking time **20–25 minutes**

1 tablespoon **sunflower oil**

3 **scallions**, sliced

½ **red bell pepper**, cored, seeded, and diced

1 **garlic clove**, finely chopped

1 inch piece of **fresh ginger root**, peeled and grated

3 teaspoons **ready-made red Thai curry paste**

1¾ cups **full-fat coconut milk**

1¾ cups **fish** or **vegetable stock** (see page 13)

2 teaspoons **Thai fish sauce**

grated zest of 1 **lime**

small bunch of **cilantro**

1 lb **mussels**, scrubbed and beards removed, any cracked or open mussels discarded

Heat the oil in a large shallow saucepan, add the scallions, red pepper, garlic, and ginger and fry for 2 minutes. Stir in the curry paste and cook for 1 minute, then mix in the coconut milk, stock, fish sauce, and lime zest. Bring to a boil and simmer for 5 minutes.

Snip half the cilantro into the soup using scissors. Add the mussels then cover and cook for 8–10 minutes until the mussels have opened.

Scoop the mussels out of the soup with a slotted spoon and put onto a large plate. Discard any shut mussels then reserve half the opened mussels in their shells for garnish. Take the remaining mussels out of their shells and stir them back into the soup. Ladle the soup into bowls, top with the reserved mussels in shells, and garnish with the remaining snipped cilantro. Serve with warm crusty bread for dunking into the soup.

For saffron mussel soup, fry 3 sliced scallions, 2 cloves finely chopped garlic, ½–1 seeded and finely chopped large mild red chili according to taste, ½ a red bell pepper and ½ a yellow or orange bell pepper, seeded and diced in 1 tablespoon olive oil until softened. Add 3 large pinches of saffron threads, ⅔ cup white wine, and 3 cups fish or vegetable stock. Season with salt and pepper and simmer for 5 minutes. Add the mussels as above then cover and simmer until the shells have opened. Serve in shallow bowls garnished with snipped parsley.

crab bisque

Serves **6**

Preparation time **20 minutes**

Cooking time **25 minutes**

2 tablespoons **butter**

1 **onion**, roughly chopped

2 tablespoons **brandy**

3 tablespoons **long-grain rice**

1¼ cups **fish stock** (see page 13)

5 oz **prepared crab on the shell**, plus **1 extra crab**, to garnish (optional)

2 canned **anchovy fillets**, drained and chopped

½ teaspoon **mild paprika**

¾ cup **milk**

⅔ cup **heavy cream**

salt and **cayenne pepper**

Heat the butter in a saucepan, add the onion, and fry gently for 5 minutes until softened. Add the brandy and when boiling, flame with a long match and quickly stand back. As soon as the flames have subsided stir in the rice and add the stock.

Scoop the dark and white crab meat out of the shell into the pan and then mix in the chopped anchovies and paprika. Season with a little salt and cayenne pepper then bring to a boil. Cover and simmer for 20 minutes.

Allow the soup to cool slightly then puree in batches in a blender or food processor. Pour back into the saucepan and stir in the milk and cream. Reheat, but take care to bring just to a boil and then reduce the heat to a simmer, stirring until hot all the way through. Taste and adjust the seasoning if needed.

Pour into teacups. Pick out the crab meat from the extra crab (if using) and flake into pieces. Serve in a separate bowl for diners to sprinkle over their soup and garnish with a little extra paprika.

For crab & salmon chowder, fry the onion in butter as above. Add 2 cups diced potato and fry for 5 minutes. Add 2 tablespoons brandy and flame as above. Mix in 2½ cups fish stock, the dark and white crab meat, anchovies, and paprika as above. Cover and simmer for 15 minutes. Add 10 oz salmon fillet, cut into 2 thick slices, cover, and simmer for 10 minutes. Lift out the salmon, peel off the skin, break into flakes, and discard any bones. Return the salmon to the soup, stir in ¾ cup milk and ⅔ cup heavy cream. Reheat and serve.

spinach soup with haddock

Serves **6**
Preparation time **30 minutes**
Cooking time **about 1 hour**

2 tablespoons **butter**
1 **onion**, roughly chopped
1 **baking potato**, about 8 oz,
    diced
4 cups **vegetable** or **chicken**
    stock (see pages 13
    and 10)
¼ teaspoon **grated nutmeg**
5 cups **young spinach**
    leaves, rinsed and drained
1¼ cups **milk**
13 oz **smoked haddock**
9 **quail's eggs**
2 **egg yolks**
⅔ cup **heavy cream**
salt and **pepper**

Heat the butter in a saucepan, add the onion, and fry gently for 5 minutes until softened. Add the potato, cover, and cook for 10 minutes, stirring occasionally.

Pour in the stock, add the nutmeg and salt and pepper then bring to a boil. Cover and simmer for 20 minutes until the potato is soft. Reserve a few tiny spinach leaves and add the rest to the pan. Re-cover the pan and cook for 5 minutes until just wilted.

Puree the soup in batches in a blender or food processor until smooth, then pour back into the saucepan, mix in the milk, and set aside.

Cut the haddock into two pieces, cook in a steamer for 8–10 minutes until the fish flakes when pressed with a knife. Put the quail's eggs into a small saucepan of cold water, bring to a boil and simmer for 2–3 minutes, drain, rinse with cold water, and peel off shells.

Mix the 2 hen egg yolks with the heavy cream. Stir into the soup and bring just to a boil, still stirring. Taste and adjust the seasoning if needed. Flake the fish, discarding the skin and bones, make small mounds in the base of 6 shallow serving bowls, and top with the quail's egg halves. Ladle the soup around the fish and eggs and garnish with tiny spinach leaves and pepper.

For cream of nettle soup, make up the soup as above using 5 cups young nettle tops instead of the spinach. (Pick nettles using rubber gloves so that you don't get stung and rinse the leaves well in cold water.) Puree the soup in a blender or food processor and finish with milk, egg yolks, and cream, as above. Garnish with diced smoked ham.

smooth carrot soup with mint oil

Serves **6**

Preparation time **20 minutes**

Cooking time **1–1¼ hours**

2 tablespoons **olive oil**

1 **onion**, roughly chopped

1½ lb **carrots**, diced

3 tablespoons **long-grain rice**

4 cups **vegetable** or **chicken
stock** (see pages 13
and 10)

1¼ cups **milk**

Mint oil

½ oz **fresh mint**

¼ teaspoon **superfine sugar**

3 tablespoons **olive oil**

salt and **pepper**

Heat the oil in a saucepan, add the onion, and fry for 5 minutes until just beginning to soften and turn golden around the edges. Stir in the carrots and cook for 5 minutes. Mix in the rice, stock, and a little salt and pepper. Bring to a boil then cover and simmer for 45 minutes, stirring occasionally until the carrots are tender.

Meanwhile make the mint oil. Strip the leaves from the mint stems and add the leaves to a blender or food processor with the sugar and a little pepper. Finely chop then gradually blend in the oil a little at a time with the motor running. Spoon into a small bowl and stir before using.

Rinse the blender or food processor, then puree the soup in batches until smooth. Return the soup to the saucepan and stir in the milk. Reheat then taste and adjust the seasoning if needed. Ladle into bowls then drizzle with the mint oil and add some extra mint leaves if desired. Serve with muffins.

For zucchini muffins, to serve as an accompaniment, put 2½ cups self-rising flour into a bowl, and add 3 teaspoons baking powder, ¾ cup freshly grated Parmesan cheese, 7 oz coarsely grated zucchini, ⅔ cup low-fat plain yogurt, 3 tablespoons olive oil, 3 eggs, and 3 tablespoons milk. Fork together until just mixed, and divide into a 12-cup muffin pan lined with paper bake cups. Bake in a preheated oven, 400°F, for 18–20 minutes until well risen and golden brown. Serve warm.

clam, potato, & bean soup

Serves **6**
Preparation time **30 minutes**
Cooking time **45 minutes**

2 tablespoons **olive oil**
4 oz piece of **unsmoked pancetta**, diced
1 **onion**, chopped
3 cups diced **potatoes**
1 **leek**, sliced
2 **garlic cloves**, crushed
1 tablespoon chopped **rosemary**
2 **bay leaves**
13 oz can **cannellini beans**, drained
3¾ cups **vegetable stock** (see page 13)
2 lb small **clams** or **mussels**, scrubbed
salt and **pepper**

Garlic & parsley oil
⅔ cup **extra virgin olive oil**
2 large **garlic cloves**, sliced
¼ teaspoon **salt**
1 tablespoon chopped **parsley**

Heat the oil in a large saucepan and fry the pancetta for 5 minutes until golden. Remove from the pan with a slotted spoon and set aside. Add the onion, potatoes, leek, garlic, rosemary, and bay leaves to the pan and fry gently for 10 minutes until softened. Add the beans and stock, bring to a boil, and simmer gently for 20 minutes, until the vegetables are tender.

Meanwhile, make the garlic and parsley oil. Heat the oil with the garlic and salt in a small pan and simmer gently for 3 minutes. Allow to cool, then stir in the parsley. Set aside.

Transfer half of the soup to a blender or food processor and puree until really smooth, then pour it back into the pan and season with salt and pepper. Stir in the clams or mussels and return the pancetta to the soup. Simmer gently until the shellfish are open, about 5 minutes (discard any that remain closed). Spoon the soup into bowls and drizzle with the garlic and parsley oil and serve with some crusty bread.

For clam, tomato, & bean soup, fry 4 oz diced chorizo in the oil instead of the pancetta, then drain and reserve. Fry the onion, potato, leek, garlic, and herbs, then add 4 large diced tomatoes (skinning them first if preferred), the beans, and stock. Simmer for 20 minutes. Puree half the soup then add the shellfish and fried chorizo and cook and serve as above with the garlic and parsley oil.

chicken & tarragon with puff pastry

Serves **6**
Preparation time **40 minutes**
Cooking time **about 1¾ hours**

6 **chicken thighs**
1 **carrot**, sliced
2 **celery sticks**, sliced
7 oz **leeks**, sliced thinly, white and green parts kept separate
3¾ cups **chicken stock** (see page 10)
¾ cup **white wine**
¼ cup **butter**
¼ cup **all-purpose flour**
grated zest of ½ **orange**
2 teaspoons **Dijon mustard**
1 tablespoon chopped **tarragon**
14 oz **frozen pack ready-rolled puff pastry sheets**, defrosted
1 **egg**, beaten, to glaze
salt and **pepper**

Put the chicken thighs into a large saucepan with the carrot, celery, and white sliced leeks. Pour on the stock, wine, salt, and pepper. Bring to a boil, then cover and simmer gently for 1 hour until the chicken is very tender.

Strain the chicken stock into a measuring cup, drain the chicken and vegetables then transfer the chicken to a cutting board and cut the meat into small pieces discarding the skin and bones and vegetables. If the stock measures more than 3¾ cups return it to the saucepan and boil rapidly until reduced.

Melt the butter in a smaller saucepan, add the green sliced leeks, and fry for 2–3 minutes until softened. Stir in the flour and cook briefly, then gradually mix in the strained stock and bring to a boil, stirring until the sauce has thickened slightly. Stir in the orange zest, mustard, and tarragon. Taste and adjust the seasoning if needed. Divide the diced chicken between 6 x 1¼ cup ovenproof dishes so that the soup three-quarter fills the dishes (any more and they will overflow during baking).

Unroll the pastry, cut 6 circles slightly larger than the tops of the dishes, then 6 long strips about ½ inch wide from the trimmings. Brush the dish rims with a little egg, stick the pastry strips around the rims, then brush these with egg before sticking the pastry lids in place. Flute the edges of the pastry with a small knife then slash the lids lightly. Brush with egg, sprinkle with a little salt, and bake in a preheated oven, 400°F, for 20–25 minutes until golden and the soup is bubbling underneath. Stand the dishes on small plates and serve immediately.

venison, red wine, & lentil soup

Serves **6**
Preparation time **20 minutes**
Cooking time **about 1½ hours**

6 **venison sausages**
1 tablespoon **olive oil**
1 **onion**, roughly chopped
2 **garlic cloves**, finely
  chopped
2 cups diced **potatoes**
1 **carrot**, diced
4 **tomatoes**, skinned if
  desired, roughly chopped
½ cup **green lentils**
1¼ cups **red wine**
6 cups **beef** or **pheasant
  stock** (see pages 12
  and 11)
2 tablespoons **cranberry
  sauce**
1 tablespoon **tomato paste**
1 teaspoon **ground allspice**
thyme sprig
2 **bay leaves**
salt and **pepper**

Broil the sausages until browned and just cooked. Meanwhile heat the oil in a large saucepan, add the onion, and fry for 5 minutes until softened and just beginning to brown. Add the garlic, potato, and carrot and fry briefly, then mix in the tomatoes and lentils.

Pour in the wine and stock, then add the cranberry sauce, tomato paste, allspice, and herbs. Season well with salt and pepper then slice the sausages and add these to the pan. Bring to a boil, stirring, then cover and simmer gently for 1¼ hours. Taste and adjust seasoning if needed.

Ladle the soup into bowls and serve with French bread croutons (see page 15) rubbed with a little garlic and sprinkled with parsley.

For pheasant, bacon, & blood sausage soup, omit the sausages, adding instead 5 oz diced smoked streaky bacon when frying the onion. Add 4 oz diced blood sausage and the leftover diced meat from a roast pheasant along with the potato, carrot, tomatoes, and lentils. Continue as above, adding pheasant stock in place of beef stock.

mushroom & madeira soup

Serves **6**
Preparation time **30 minutes**
Cooking time **40 minutes**

¼ cup **butter**
1 tablespoon **olive oil**
1 **onion**, chopped
13 oz **cup mushrooms**, sliced
2 large **flat mushrooms**,
  sliced
2 **garlic cloves**, finely
  chopped
½ cup **Madeira or medium
  sherry**
3¾ cups **chicken** or
  vegetable stock (see
  pages 10 and 13)
3 tablespoons **long-grain rice**
2 **thyme sprigs**
1¾ cups **milk**
⅔ cup **heavy cream**
salt and **pepper**

To garnish
2 tablespoons **butter**
8 oz package **exotic
  mushrooms**
few extra **thyme leaves**

Heat the butter and oil in a large saucepan, add the onion, and fry gently for 5 minutes until just turning golden around the edges. Add the mushrooms and garlic and fry over a high heat for 2–3 minutes until golden.

Stir in the Madeira, stock, rice, and thyme, then season with salt and pepper and bring to a boil. Cover and simmer for 30 minutes.

Allow the soup to cool slightly and discard the thyme sprigs. Puree the soup in batches in a blender or food processor until smooth. Return to the saucepan and stir in the milk and cream. Reheat without boiling, then taste and adjust the seasoning if needed.

Make the garnish by heating the remaining butter in a skillet and slicing any large exotic mushrooms, then add them to the pan and fry for 2 minutes until golden. Ladle the soup into shallow soup bowls and gently spoon the mushrooms into the center. Garnish with a few thyme leaves and serve with scones (see below).

For baby walnut scones, to serve as an accompaniment, blend ¼ cup butter into 2 cups self-rising flour. Season and mix in ⅓ cup roughly chopped walnuts, 2 teaspoons thyme leaves, and ¾ cup grated sharp cheddar cheese. Mix in ½ a beaten egg and 8–10 tablespoons milk to make a soft dough. Knead lightly, then roll out to 1 inch thickness. Stamp out 2 inch circles. Put on a greased baking sheet, brush with remaining ½ egg, then bake in a preheated oven, 400°F, for 10–12 minutes. Serve warm.

chestnut soup with truffle oil

Serves **6**

Preparation time **30 minutes**

Cooking time **1¼ hours**

1 lb **fresh chestnuts**

¼ cup **butter**

1 **onion**, finely chopped

10 **bacon slices**

2 cups diced **potatoes**

4 tablespoons **brandy**, plus a
   little extra to serve

3¾ cups **pheasant** or **beef
   stock** (see pages 11
   and 12)

fresh thyme sprig

large pinch of **ground
   cinnamon**

large pinch of **grated nutmeg**

salt and **pepper**

little **truffle oil**, to garnish
   (optional)

Make a cross cut in the top of each chestnut then add to a saucepan of boiling water and poach for 15 minutes. Drain into a colander, rinse with cold water so that they are cool enough to handle, then remove the skins with a small sharp knife and roughly chop.

Heat the butter in a saucepan, add the onion, and fry gently for 5 minutes until just beginning to turn golden around the edges. Dice 4 slices of the bacon and add to the pan along with the potato and chestnuts. Fry gently for 5 minutes, stirring occasionally.

Add the brandy and, when bubbling, flame with a long taper and quickly stand back. As soon as the flames have subsided pour in the stock. Add the thyme, spices, and seasoning and bring to a boil, cover, and simmer for 45 minutes.

Discard the thyme sprig and puree half the soup in a blender or food processor until smooth. Return to the soup in the pan and reheat. Taste and adjust the seasoning if needed. Wrap each remaining slice of bacon around a skewer and broil until crisp. Ladle the soup into cups and top with the bacon skewers. Drizzle with the truffle oil and a little extra brandy if desired.

For walnut & celeriac soup, fry the onion in butter as above. Add 4 diced bacon slices, 12 oz peeled and diced celeriac instead of the potato, and 1¾ cups walnut pieces. Fry gently for 5 minutes. Omit the brandy, stir in the stock, thyme, and spices and simmer for 45 minutes. Puree and add a little extra stock if needed. Reheat and serve with croutons (see page 15).

corn & celery soup

Serves **6**

Preparation time **25 minutes**

Cooking time **30 minutes**

¼ cup **butter**

1 **onion**, chopped

4 **corn ears**, green leaves
removed, kernels cut from
cobs

3 **celery sticks**, sliced

2 **garlic cloves**, finely
chopped

4 cups **chicken** or **vegetable
stock** (see pages 10
and 13)

2 **bay leaves**

salt and **cayenne pepper**

Heat the butter in a saucepan, add the onion, and fry gently for 5 minutes until just beginning to turn golden around the edges. Add the corn, celery, and garlic and fry for 5 minutes.

Pour in the stock, add the bay leaves, salt, and pepper and bring to a boil. Cover and simmer for 20 minutes.

Discard the bay leaves then allow the soup to cool slightly. Puree the soup in batches in a blender or food processor until smooth. Return to the saucepan and reheat. Taste and adjust the seasoning if needed. Ladle into bowls and top with spoonfuls of chili and tomato chutney (see below).

For chili & tomato chutney, to serve as an accompaniment, heat 1 tablespoon sunflower oil in a small saucepan, add ½ a finely chopped red onion, 1 cored, seeded, and diced red bell pepper and 1–2 large mild, cored, seeded, and finely chopped red chilies, to taste. Fry gently for 5 minutes until softened, then mix in 4 chopped tomatoes (skinned if desired), 4 tablespoons superfine sugar, 2 tablespoons red wine vinegar, and a little salt and pepper. Simmer for 15 minutes, stirring occasionally until thick.

lentil, pancetta, & scallop soup

Serves **4**

Preparation time **15 minutes**

Cooking time **about 40 minutes**

¼ cup **puy lentils**

1 tablespoon **olive oil**

1 small **leek**, diced

3 oz diced **pancetta**

1 **garlic clove**, finely chopped

4 tablespoons **Pernod**

2½ cups **fish stock** (see page 13)

grated zest of ½ **lemon**

⅔ cup **heavy cream**

small bunch of **parsley**

2 tablespoons **butter**

7 oz bag **frozen baby scallops**, defrosted

salt and **pepper**

Bring a saucepan of water to a boil, add the lentils, and simmer for 20 minutes until just tender. Drain into a sieve, rinse and drain again, and set aside. Wash and dry the pan.

Heat the oil in the cleaned pan then add the leek, pancetta, and garlic and fry for 5 minutes, stirring until the pancetta is just beginning to turn golden. Add the Pernod and, when bubbling, flame with a long taper and quickly stand well back. As soon as the flames subside pour in the stock. Add the lemon zest and a little salt and pepper, then bring to a boil and simmer uncovered for 10 minutes.

Stir in the cooked lentils, cream, and parsley, then taste and adjust the seasoning if needed. Heat the butter in a skillet. Rinse the scallops in cold water and drain well, then add to the pan and fry for 3–4 minutes, turning until golden and cooked through.

Ladle the soup into shallow bowls and spoon the scallops into a small mound in the center.

For creamy pancetta & mussel soup, make up the soup as above. When the stock has cooked for 10 minutes, add 1 lb closed mussels that have been scrubbed and had their beards removed. Cover and simmer for 8–10 minutes until the mussels have opened. Discard any that are still closed then spoon into bowls. Stir the cream and parsley into the soup, then ladle over the mussels.

five-spice duck soup & bok choy

Serves **4**
Preparation time **15 minutes**
Cooking time **20 minutes**

5 cups **duck stock** (see
page 11)
grated zest and juice of
1 **orange**
4 tablespoons **medium
sherry**
¼ teaspoon **five-spice
powder**
2 inch piece of **fresh ginger
root**, thinly sliced
1 tablespoon **soy sauce**
2 tablespoons **Chinese plum
sauce**
4–6 oz **leftover cooked duck**,
stripped from carcass before
stock was made
½ bunch of **scallions**, thinly
sliced
2 **bok choy**, thickly sliced
salt and **pepper** (optional)

Pour the stock into a saucepan then add the orange
zest and juice, sherry, spice powder, and ginger. Stir in
the soy sauce and plum sauce then bring to a boil,
stirring. Cover and simmer gently for 15 minutes.

Add the duck, scallions, and bok choy and simmer for
5 minutes. Taste and add a little salt and pepper if
needed then ladle into bowls.

For herbed duck broth with noodles, soak 2 oz fine
dried egg noodles in boiling water for 5 minutes. Heat
5 cups duck stock as above and substitute the orange
zest and juice with that of ½ a lemon. Omit the sherry
and spice powder, but add the ginger and soy sauce,
cover, and simmer as above. Add 3 tablespoons fresh
chopped parsley and 3 tablespoons fresh chopped
mint, then add the leftover cooked shredded duck,
salt, and pepper and simmer for 5 minutes. Divide the
noodles between the bowls and ladle the broth over
the top.

salmon & tarragon sabayon

Serves **6**
Preparation time **10 minutes**
Cooking time **15 minutes**

13 oz **salmon**, cut into two
4 tablespoons **Noilly Prat**
4 **scallions**, thinly sliced, white
  and green parts kept
  separate
pared zest of **1 lemon**
2½ cups **fish stock** (see
  page 13)
4 **egg yolks**
1 tablespoon finely chopped
  fresh **tarragon**
1 teaspoon **Dijon mustard**
2 tablespoons **butter**, at room
  temperature
⅔ cup **heavy cream**
salt and **pepper**
tarragon sprigs, to garnish
  (optional)

Put the salmon pieces into a saucepan with the Noilly Prat, white sliced scallions, lemon zest, and the stock. Season with salt and pepper and bring to a boil. Cover and simmer for 10 minutes until the fish is cooked and flakes easily when pressed with a knife.

Lift the fish out of the stock and break into pieces, carefully checking for any bones. Keep hot under foil.

Beat the egg yolks, tarragon, mustard, and butter together in a large bowl. Strain the stock, then gradually beat it into the egg mixture until smooth. Pour into the saucepan, add the cream and green sliced scallions, then beat over a low heat for 4–5 minutes until the mixture is frothy and slightly thickened. Take care not to overheat the soup or the eggs will curdle. Taste and adjust the seasoning if needed.

Divide the salmon flakes between 6 shallow serving bowls, pour the hot frothy sabayon around the salmon, and garnish with tarragon sprigs, if desired. Serve with melba toast.

For melba toast, to serve as an accompaniment, lightly toast 4 slices of bread on both sides. Trim off the crusts then cut in half horizontally through the bread to make 8 very thin slices. Cut the slices into triangles then put onto a baking sheet, untoasted side upward and broil until the corners of the bread begin to curl.

vegetable broth with wontons

Serves **6**

Preparation time **40 minutes**,
 plus marinading

Cooking time **5 minutes**

Wontons

4 oz **ground pork**

½ teaspoon **cornstarch**

1 teaspoon **sesame oil**

2 tablespoons **soy sauce**

1 small **garlic clove**, finely
 chopped

1¾ oz can **dark crab meat**

1 **egg**, separated

18 x 3¾ inch square **wonton
 wrappers**

Broth

5 cups **chicken stock** (see
 page 10)

1 bunch **asparagus**, trimmed,
 thickly sliced

3 oz **snow peas**, sliced

4 **scallions**, thinly sliced

4 teaspoons **fish sauce**

4 tablespoons **dry sherry**

small bunch of **cilantro**, two-
 thirds roughly chopped, the
 remaining sprigs to garnish

Mix all the wonton ingredients together except the egg
white and wrappers and chill for 30 minutes for the
flavors to develop. Separate the wonton wrappers, add
a heaping teaspoonful of the pork mixture onto each,
brush the edges of the wrapper with a little egg white,
then bring the edges up and over the filling and twist
together to make mini parcels.

Put all the broth ingredients into a large saucepan,
bring to a boil then add the wontons and simmer for
5 minutes until the filling is cooked through. Ladle into
bowls and garnish with cilantro sprigs.

For vegetable broth with chilied tuna, make up
the broth as above but omit the wontons. Rub a
7 oz thick cut tuna steak with 1 teaspoon sesame
oil and 1 teaspoon sunflower oil, 1 seeded and finely
chopped red chili, and 1 finely chopped garlic clove.
Add to a preheated skillet and fry for 1½ minutes
each side until the top and bottom are browned and
the center still pink. Thinly slice and divide between
soup bowls. Ladle the broth around the tuna and
serve immediately otherwise the soup will overcook
the tuna.

chorizo, fennel, & potato soup

Serves **8–10**
Preparation time **15 minutes**
Cooking time **30 minutes**

3 tablespoons **olive oil**
1 **onion**, chopped
13 oz **fennel bulb**, chopped
5 oz **chorizo**, cut into small
   pieces
1 lb floury **potatoes**, cut into
   small dice
4 cups **chicken** or **ham stock**
   (see page 10)
3 tablespoons finely chopped
   cilantro
3 tablespoons **sour cream**
salt and **pepper**

Heat the oil in a large saucepan and gently fry the onion and fennel for about 10 minutes until they are very soft and beginning to brown.

Add the chorizo, potatoes, and stock and bring to a boil. Reduce the heat, cover with a lid, and cook gently for 20 minutes until the potatoes are very tender.

Blend the soup until fairly smooth in a blender or food processor. Stir in the cilantro and sour cream and heat through gently for a couple of minutes. Season with salt and pepper to taste and serve in small, warmed cups.

For chorizo, celery, & potato soup, fry the onion in the oil as above, adding 2 cups chopped celery instead of the fennel. Continue as the recipe but serve without pureeing, stirring the cilantro and sour cream through just before serving.

158

healthy
soups

pesto & lemon soup

Serves **6**

Preparation time **10 minutes**

Cooking time **25 minutes**

1 tablespoon **olive oil**

1 **onion**, finely chopped

2 **garlic cloves**, finely chopped

2 **tomatoes**, skinned, chopped

5 cups **vegetable stock** (see page 13)

3 teaspoons **pesto**, plus extra to serve

grated zest and juice of 1 **lemon**

4 oz **broccoli**, cut into small florets, stems sliced

5 oz **zucchini**, diced

½ cup **frozen green soy beans**

2½ oz small **pasta shapes**

1 cup **spinach**, shredded

salt and **pepper**

fresh **basil leaves**, to garnish (optional)

Heat the oil in a saucepan, add the onion, and fry gently for 5 minutes, stirring occasionally until softened. Add the garlic, tomatoes, stock, pesto, lemon zest, and a little salt and pepper and simmer gently for 10 minutes.

Add the broccoli, zucchini, soy beans, and pasta shapes, then simmer for 6 minutes. Add the spinach and lemon juice and cook for 2 minutes until the spinach has just wilted and the pasta is cooked.

Ladle into bowls, top with extra spoonfuls of pesto, and garnish with a sprinkling of basil leaves. Serve with warm olive or sundried tomato focaccia or ciabatta bread or Parmesan thins.

For homemade Parmesan thins, to serve as an accompaniment, line a baking sheet with nonstick parchment paper then sprinkle 1 cup freshly grated Parmesan cheese into 18 well-spaced mounds. Cook in a preheated oven, 375°F, for about 5 minutes, or until the cheese has melted and is just beginning to brown. Allow to cool and harden, then peel off the paper and serve on the side with the soup.

seafood gumbo

Serves **6**

Preparation time **20 minutes**

Cooking time **30 minutes**

1 tablespoon **sunflower oil**

1 **onion**, finely chopped

1 small **carrot**, diced

1 **celery stick**, diced

½ **red bell pepper**, cored, seeded, and diced

14 oz **tomatoes**, skinned if desired, roughly chopped

large **thyme sprig**

¼ teaspoon **dried red pepper flakes**

2 teaspoons **tomato paste**

4 cups **vegetable** or **fish stock** (see page 13)

3 tablespoons **long-grain rice**

13 oz package **frozen seafood selection**, defrosted, rinsed with cold water, and drained

1½ oz can **dressed crab**

½ cup sliced **okra**

salt and **pepper**

few extra **thyme leaves**, to garnish (optional)

Heat the oil in a saucepan, add the onion, and fry gently for 5 minutes until softened and just beginning to brown. Stir in the carrot, celery, and red pepper and fry for a few more minutes. Mix in the tomatoes, thyme, red pepper flakes, and tomato paste, then pour in the stock. Add the rice, season with salt and pepper, and bring to a boil.

Cover and simmer for 20 minutes, stirring occasionally. Halve any very large mussels, then stir into the soup with the remaining seafood, canned crab, and okra. Cover and simmer for 5 minutes, then taste and adjust the seasoning if needed. Ladle into bowls and sprinkle with a few thyme leaves, if desired. Serve with crusty bread.

For chicken & ham gumbo, fry 6 diced, skinned, and boned chicken thighs along with the onion. Continue making the soup as above, adding in 2 oz diced ham and 1 cup sliced green beans instead of the seafood, crab, and okra. Finish and serve as above.

summer vegetable soup

Serves **4**

Preparation time **15 minutes**

Cooking time **about 25 minutes**

1 teaspoon **olive oil**

1 **leek**, finely sliced

1 large **potato**, peeled and chopped

1 lb **mixed summer vegetables** (such as peas, asparagus, fava beans, and zucchini)

2 tablespoons chopped **mint**

3¾ cups **vegetable stock** (see page 13)

2 tablespoons sour cream

salt and **pepper**

Heat the oil in a medium saucepan and fry the leek for 3–4 minutes until softened.

Add the potato and stock to the pan and cook for 10 minutes. Add all the remaining vegetables and the mint, then bring to a boil. Reduce the heat and simmer for 10 minutes.

Transfer the soup to a blender or food processor and puree until smooth. Return the soup to the pan, add the sour cream and season to taste with salt and pepper. Heat through gently and serve.

For chunky summer vegetable soup with mixed herb gremolata, make up the soup as above but do not puree. Ladle the soup into bowls and serve topped with 2 tablespoons of sour cream and gremolata made by mixing 2 tablespoons chopped basil, 2 tablespoons chopped parsley, the grated zest of 1 lemon, and 1 small finely chopped garlic clove.

cheat's curried vegetable soup

Serves **6**
Preparation time **25 minutes**
Cooking time **40 minutes**

2 tablespoons **sunflower oil**
1 **onion**, finely chopped
2 **garlic cloves**, finely chopped
4 teaspoons **ready-made
    mild curry paste**
1 inch piece of **fresh ginger
    root**, peeled and grated
2 small **baking potatoes**, diced
2 **carrots**, diced
1 small **cauliflower**, core
    discarded, florets cut into
    small pieces
¾ cup **red lentils**
6 cups **vegetable** or **chicken
    stock** (see pages 13
    and 10)
13 oz can **chopped tomatoes**
5 cups **spinach leaves**, rinsed
    and any large leaves torn
    into pieces

Raita
⅔ cup **low-fat plain yogurt**
4 tablespoons chopped
    cilantro leaves
4 teaspoons **mango chutney**

Heat the oil in a large saucepan, add the onion, and fry for 5 minutes, stirring until softened. Stir in the garlic, curry paste, and ginger and cook for 1 minute.

Mix in the potatoes, carrots, cauliflower, and lentils. Pour in the stock and tomatoes, season with salt and pepper, and bring to a boil. Cover and simmer for 30 minutes or until the lentils are tender.

Meanwhile, mix the yogurt, cilantro, and mango chutney together to make the raita and spoon into a small bowl.

Add the spinach to the soup and cook for 2 minutes until just wilted. Taste and adjust the seasoning if needed. Ladle the soup into shallow bowls, top with spoonfuls of raita. Serve with warmed naan breads, if desired.

For curried eggplant soup, fry the onion with 2 diced eggplants until the eggplants are lightly browned. Stir in the garlic, curry paste, and ginger and cook as above. Add the potatoes, carrots, lentils, stock, and tomatoes, omitting the cauliflower. After 30 minutes simmering, puree the soup in a blender or food processor then reheat. Omit the spinach, serve with a swirl of plain yogurt, a little chopped cilantro, and pappadams.

red pepper & zucchini soup

Serves **4**
Preparation time **15 minutes**
Cooking time **about 40
minutes**

2 tablespoons **olive oil**
2 **onions**, finely chopped
1 **garlic clove**, crushed
3 **red bell peppers**, cored,
seeded, and roughly
chopped
2 **zucchini**, roughly chopped
3¾ cups **vegetable stock**
(see page 13) or **water**
salt and **pepper**

To serve
low-fat plain yogurt or **sour
cream**
whole chives

Heat the oil in a large saucepan and fry the onions
gently for 5 minutes, or until softened and golden
brown. Add the garlic and cook gently for 1 minute.
Add the peppers and half the zucchini to the pan. Fry
for 5–8 minutes, or until softened and brown.

Add the stock to the pan, season to taste with salt and
pepper, and bring to a boil. Reduce the heat, cover the
pan, and simmer gently for 20 minutes.

Allow the soup to cool slightly once the vegetables are
tender, then puree in batches in a blender or food
processor. Gently fry the remaining chopped zucchini
for 5 minutes. Meanwhile, return the soup to the pan,
reheat, taste, and adjust the seasoning if needed. Serve
topped with the fried zucchini, yogurt, or sour cream
and chives.

For red pepper & carrot soup, make up the soup
as above, adding 2 diced carrots instead of the
zucchini, plus the peppers, to the fried onion and
garlic. Continue as above. Puree, reheat, and serve
topped with 8 teaspoonfuls of garlic and herb soft
cheese and some chopped chives.

fennel seed root vegetable soup

Serves **6**

Preparation time **25 minutes**

Cooking time **about 50 minutes**

1 tablespoon **olive oil**

1 **onion**, roughly chopped

2 **garlic cloves**, roughly chopped

2 teaspoons **fennel seeds**, roughly crushed

½ teaspoon **smoked paprika**

½ teaspoon **turmeric**

8 oz **carrots**, diced

8 oz **parsnips**, diced

8 oz **rutabaga**, diced

4 cups **vegetable** or **chicken stock** (see pages 13 and 10)

1¼ cups **skim milk**

salt and **pepper**

Heat the oil in a large saucepan, add the onion, and fry for 5 minutes until just beginning to soften. Stir in the garlic, fennel seeds, and spices and cook for 1 minute to release their flavor.

Add the root vegetables, stock, salt, and pepper and bring to a boil. Cover and simmer for 45 minutes, stirring occasionally, until the vegetables are very tender. Allow to cool slightly, then puree in batches in a blender or food processor until smooth.

Pour the puree back into the saucepan and stir in the milk. Reheat then taste and adjust the seasoning if needed. Ladle into bowls and serve with croutons (see page 15).

For low-fat spiced croutons, to serve as an accompaniment, cut 3 slices of whole-wheat bread into cubes, put on a baking sheet, squirt with spray olive oil 3 or 4 times, then sprinkle with 1 teaspoon roughly crushed fennel seeds, ¼ teaspoon smoked paprika, and ¼ teaspoon turmeric. Bake in a preheated oven, 375°F, for 15 minutes until crisp.

tomato & orange soup

Serves **6**

Preparation time **15 minutes**

Cooking time **about 40 minutes**

2 tablespoons **olive oil**

1 **onion**, roughly chopped

2 **garlic cloves**, crushed

4 lb **ripe tomatoes**, skinned and chopped

2 tablespoons **tomato paste**

1¾ cups **vegetable** or **chicken stock** (see pages 13 and 10)

grated zest of 1 large **orange**

5 tablespoons **orange juice**

4 **basil sprigs**

1–2 teaspoons **brown sugar**

salt and **pepper**

To garnish

2–3 tablespoons finely chopped **basil**

⅔ cup **low-fat Greek or plain yogurt**

6 small **basil sprigs**

thin strips of **orange rind**

Heat the oil in a large saucepan and fry the onion and garlic until softened. Add the tomatoes, tomato paste, stock, orange zest and juice, and basil. Bring to a boil, then reduce the heat, cover the pan, and simmer gently for 20–25 minutes until the vegetables are soft.

Allow the soup to cool slightly, then puree in batches in a blender or food processor and push through a nylon sieve into the rinsed pan to remove the seeds. Season with salt, pepper, and a little sugar. Return the pan to the heat and bring to a boil, then add a little extra stock or tomato juice if necessary to achieve the desired consistency.

Fold the chopped basil gently into the yogurt. Pour the hot soup into warmed soup plates, spoon a little basil yogurt on each one, and garnish with small basil sprigs and orange rind.

For tomato soup with crispy chorizo, make up the soup as above, omitting the orange zest and juice, adding 5 tablespoons red wine instead. Puree and serve topped with 1½ oz ready sliced chorizo, dry-fried until browned, then diced.

cauliflower & cumin soup

Serves **4**
Preparation time **15 minutes**
Cooking time **about 20
 minutes**

2 teaspoons **sunflower oil**
1 **onion**, chopped
1 **garlic clove**, crushed
2 teaspoons **cumin seeds**
1 **cauliflower**, cut into florets
1 large **potato**, peeled and
 chopped
1¾ cups **vegetable stock**
 (see page 13)
1¾ cups **low-fat milk**
2 tablespoons **low-fat sour
 cream**
2 tablespoons chopped
 cilantro leaves
salt and **pepper**

Heat the oil in a medium saucepan and fry the onion, garlic, and cumin seeds for 3–4 minutes. Add the cauliflower, potato, stock, and milk and bring to a boil. Reduce the heat and simmer for 15 minutes.

Transfer the soup to a blender or food processor and puree until smooth. Stir through the sour cream and cilantro and season to taste with salt and pepper. Heat through and serve with slices of crusty whole-wheat bread.

For curried cauliflower soup, fry the onion and garlic in the oil as above, omitting the cumin. Stir in 2 tablespoons mild curry paste, cook for 1 minute, then add the cauliflower, potato, stock, and milk. Continue as the recipe above. Serve with some tiny circular pappadams.

fennel & lemon soup

Serves **4**
Preparation time **20 minutes**
Cooking time **about 25 minutes**

3 tablespoons **olive oil**
3 large **scallions**, chopped
8 oz **fennel bulb**, trimmed, cored, and finely sliced
1 **potato**, peeled and diced
finely grated zest and juice of 1 **lemon**
3¾ cups **chicken** or **vegetable stock** (see pages 10 and 13)
salt and **pepper**

Black olive gremolata
1 small **garlic clove**, finely chopped
finely grated zest of 1 **lemon**
4 tablespoons chopped **parsley**
16 **black Greek olives**, pitted and chopped

Heat the oil in a large saucepan and fry the scallions for 5 minutes until soft. Add the fennel, potato, and lemon zest and cook for 5 minutes until the fennel begins to soften. Pour in the stock and bring to a boil. Reduce the heat, cover the pan, and simmer for about 15 minutes until the ingredients are tender.

Meanwhile, to make the gremolata, mix together the garlic, lemon zest, and parsley, then stir in the olives. Cover and chill until required.

Puree the soup in a blender or food processor and pass it through a sieve to remove any strings of fennel. The soup should not be too thick, so add more stock if necessary. Return the soup to the rinsed pan. Taste and season well with salt and pepper and lemon juice, then heat through gently. Pour the soup into warmed bowls and sprinkle with some gremolata, to be stirred in before eating. Serve with slices of toasted crusty bread, or croutons (see page 15), if desired.

For fennel & trout soup, omit the gremolata and instead steam 2 boneless trout fillets above the simmering soup for 10 minutes, until the fish flakes easily when pressed with a knife. Lift the trout out of the steamer, remove the skin then break into flakes, removing any bones. Spoon into the base of 4 shallow serving bowls then ladle the soup over the top.

roasted root vegetable soup

Serves **6**

Preparation time **10 minutes**

Cooking time **1 hour 5 minutes**

4 **carrots**, chopped

2 **parsnips**, chopped

olive oil, for spraying

1 **leek**, finely chopped

5 cups **vegetable stock** (see page 13)

2 teaspoons **thyme leaves**

salt and **pepper**

thyme sprigs, to garnish

Place the carrots and parsnips in a roasting pan, spray lightly with olive oil, and season with salt and pepper. Roast in a preheated oven, 400°F, for 1 hour or until the vegetables are very soft.

Meanwhile, 20 minutes before the vegetables have finished roasting, put the leeks in a large saucepan with the stock and 1 teaspoon of the thyme. Cover the pan and simmer for 20 minutes.

Transfer the roasted root vegetables to a blender or food processor and blend, adding a little of the stock if necessary. Transfer to the stock saucepan and season to taste. Add the remaining thyme, stir, and simmer for 5 minutes to reheat.

Ladle into individual bowls and serve garnished with the thyme sprigs.

For roasted butternut squash soup, halve, seed then peel a 1½ lb butternut squash, cut into thick slices, and put into a roasting pan. Spray with a little olive oil and season with salt and pepper. Roast at 400°F, for 45 minutes then continue as the recipe above.

red pepper & ginger soup

Serves **4**
Preparation time **20 minutes**,
  plus cooling
Cooking time **45 minutes**

3 **red bell peppers**, halved,
  cored, and seeded
1 **red onion**, quartered
2 **garlic cloves**
1 teaspoon **olive oil**
2 inch piece of **fresh ginger
  root**, grated
1 teaspoon **ground cumin**
1 teaspoon **ground coriander**
1 large **potato**, chopped
3¾ cups **vegetable stock**
  (see page 13)
4 tablespoons **plain yogurt**
salt and **pepper**

Place the peppers, onion, and garlic cloves in a nonstick roasting pan. Roast in a preheated oven, 400°F, for 40 minutes or until the peppers have blistered and the onion quarters and garlic are soft. If the onion quarters start to brown too much, cover them with the pepper halves and continue cooking.

Meanwhile, heat the oil in a saucepan and fry the ginger, cumin, and coriander over a low heat for 5 minutes until softened. Add the potato, stir well, and season to taste with salt and pepper. Add the stock, cover the pan, and simmer for 30 minutes.

Remove the roasted vegetables from the oven. Place the peppers in a plastic bag, tie the top, and allow to cool. Add the onions to the potato mixture and carefully squeeze out the garlic pulp from the skins into the saucepan. Remove the skins from the peppers and add all but one half to the soup. Simmer for 5 minutes.

Puree the soup in a food processor or blender until smooth. Return to the saucepan and thin with a little water, if necessary, to achieve the desired consistency.

Spoon into individual bowls. Slice the remaining piece of pepper and place the strips on top of the soup with a spoonful of yogurt.

For red pepper & pesto soup, roast the peppers, onion, and garlic as above. Heat the oil in a saucepan, omit the spices and add 2 teaspoons pesto sauce and the diced potato, fry gently for 2–3 minutes then continue as the recipe above.

zucchini & dill soup

Serves **8**
Preparation time **20 minutes**
Cooking time **20–25 minutes**

2 tablespoons **sunflower** or
   light olive oil
1 large **onion**, chopped
2 **garlic cloves**, crushed
2 lb **zucchini**, sliced
5–6 cups **vegetable** or
   chicken stock (see pages
   13 and 10)
2–4 tablespoons finely
   chopped **dill weed**
salt and **pepper**

To garnish
½ cup **light cream**
dill fronds

Heat the oil in a saucepan and fry the onion and garlic until soft but not browned. Add the zucchini, cover the pan with waxed paper, and cook over a low heat for 10 minutes until the zucchini are soft. Add 5 cups of the stock, cover the pan with a lid, and simmer for an additional 10–15 minutes.

Transfer the zucchini and a little of the stock to a blender or food processor. Puree until smooth, then pour into a clean saucepan. Add the stock that the zucchini were cooked in and the remaining stock, along with the chopped dill. Season to taste with salt and pepper, then bring to a boil.

Serve the soup in warmed soup bowls, garnished with a swirl of cream and dill fronds.

For mixed squash & dill soup, heat 2 tablespoons sunflower oil in a saucepan, add 1 chopped onion and 2 crushed garlic cloves, and fry for 5 minutes. Add 1 lb diced zucchini or vegetable marrow and 1 lb prepared and diced pumpkin or butternut squash (weigh after seeding and peeling). Cook gently as above, then add the stock and continue as above. Serve with garlic croutons (see page 15).

184

bean & sundried tomato soup

Serves **4**
Preparation time **5 minutes**
Cooking time **20 minutes**

3 tablespoons **extra virgin olive oil**
1 **onion**, finely chopped
2 **celery sticks**, thinly sliced
2 **garlic cloves**, thinly sliced
2 x 14 oz cans **lima beans**, drained and rinsed
4 tablespoons **sundried tomato paste**
3¾ cups **vegetable stock** (see page 13)
1 tablespoon chopped **rosemary** or **thyme**
salt and **pepper**
Parmesan cheese shavings, to garnish

Heat the oil in a saucepan. Add the onion and fry for 3 minutes until softened. Add the celery and garlic and fry for 2 minutes.

Add the lima beans, sundried tomato paste, vegetable stock, rosemary or thyme, and a little salt and pepper. Bring to a boil, then reduce the heat, cover, and simmer gently for 15 minutes. Serve sprinkled with Parmesan cheese shavings.

For chickpea, tomato, & rosemary soup, stir

2 x 14 oz cans of drained chickpeas into the fried onion, celery, and garlic mixture. Add 3 tablespoons ordinary tomato paste, 2 teaspoons harissa paste, 3¾ cups vegetable stock, and 1 tablespoon fresh chopped rosemary leaves. Cover, simmer, and serve as above.

spicy cilantro & lentil soup

Serves **8**

Preparation time **10–15 minutes**

Cooking time **40–50 minutes**

2½ cups **red lentils**

2 tablespoons **vegetable oil**

2 **onions**, chopped

2 **garlic cloves**, chopped

2 **celery sticks**, chopped

13 oz can **tomatoes**, drained

1 **chili**, seeded and chopped (optional)

1 teaspoon **paprika**

1 teaspoon **harissa paste**

1 teaspoon **ground cumin**

5 cups **vegetable stock** (see page 13)

salt and **pepper**

2 tablespoons chopped **cilantro**, to garnish

Place the lentils in a bowl of water. Heat the oil in a large saucepan and gently fry the onions, garlic, and celery over a low heat until softened.

Drain the lentils and add them to the vegetable pan with the tomatoes. Mix well. Add the chili, if using, paprika, harissa paste, cumin, and vegetable stock and season with salt and pepper. Cover the pan and simmer gently for about 40–50 minutes until the lentils are tender, adding a little more vegetable stock or water if the soup gets too thick.

Serve the soup immediately in warmed individual bowls topped with a little chopped coriander.

For spicy cilantro & white bean soup, fry the onions, garlic, and celery in the oil as above. Drain 2 x 14 oz cans of navy or cannellini beans then add to the pan with chili, flavorings, and stock as above. Simmer for 40–50 minutes then roughly mash some of the beans to thicken the soup. Finish with 2 tablespoons fresh chopped cilantro and 4 tablespoons fresh chopped parsley.

summer green pea soup

Serves **4**

Preparation time **10 minutes or longer if shelling fresh peas**

Cooking time **about 15 minutes**

1 tablespoon **butter**

bunch of **scallions**, chopped

2½ lb **fresh peas**, shelled, or 3 cups **frozen peas**

3 cups **vegetable stock** (see page 13)

2 tablespoons **thick plain yogurt** or **light cream**

nutmeg

1 tablespoon chopped and 2 whole **chives**, to garnish

Melt the butter in a large pan and soften the scallions, but do not allow them to brown. Add the peas to the pan with the stock. Bring to a boil and simmer for about 5 minutes for frozen peas, but for up to 15 minutes for fresh peas, until they are cooked. Be careful not to overcook fresh peas or they will lose their flavor.

Remove from the heat and puree in a blender or food processor. Add the yogurt or cream and grate in a little nutmeg. Reheat gently if necessary, and serve sprinkled with chives.

For minted pea & fava bean soup, fry the scallions in the butter as above then add 1¼ lb fresh peas and 1¼ lb fresh fava beans, both podded, or 1⅔ cups frozen peas and 1½ cups frozen fava beans, 2 stems of fresh mint, and the stock. Simmer as above then puree, reheat, and ladle into bowls, top with 4 tablespoons heavy cream, swirled into the soup, and a few tiny fresh mint leaves.

scallop & broccoli broth

Serves **4**
Preparation time **10 minutes**
Cooking time **about 40 minutes**

5 cups **vegetable** or **chicken stock** (see pages 13 and 10)
1 inch piece of **fresh ginger root**, peeled and cut into thin strips, peel reserved
1 tablespoon **soy sauce**
3 **scallions**, cut into fine diagonal slices
1 lb **broccoli**, trimmed and cut into small florets
1 small **red chili**, seeded and finely sliced (optional)
12 large **scallops**, with roes
few drops of **Thai fish sauce**
juice of ½ **lime**
sesame oil, to serve

Put the stock into a large saucepan with the ginger peel and boil for 15 minutes. Set aside and allow to steep for an additional 15 minutes.

Strain the stock into a clean saucepan. Add the soy sauce, strips of ginger, scallions, broccoli, and chili, if using, and simmer for 5 minutes.

Add the scallops, simmer for an additional 3 minutes, or until the scallops are just cooked through. Season with Thai fish sauce and lime juice.

Remove the scallops from the soup with a slotted spoon and put 3 in each individual soup bowl. Divide the broccoli among the bowls and pour in the hot soup. Serve immediately with a few drops of sesame oil.

For mixed seafood & broccoli broth, make up the broth as above but omitting the scallops. Tip a 7 oz frozen mixed bag of seafood including sliced squid, mussels, and shrimp that has been thoroughly defrosted into a sieve, rinse with cold water, drain again, and then add to the broth. Simmer for 3–4 minutes until piping hot then ladle into bowls.

around
the world

scottish cullen skink

Serves **6**
Preparation time **25 minutes**
Cooking time **40 minutes**

2 tablespoons **butter**
1 **onion**, roughly chopped
1 lb **potatoes**, diced
1 large **Finnan haddock**
  or 10 oz **smoked**
  haddock fillet
1 **bay leaf**
3¾ cups **fish stock** (see
  page 13)
⅔ cup **milk**
6 tablespoons **heavy cream**
salt and **pepper**
chopped **parsley**, to garnish

Heat the butter in a saucepan, add the onion, and fry gently for 5 minutes until softened. Stir the potatoes into the butter and onion then cover and cook for 5 more minutes. Lay the haddock on top, add the bay leaf and stock. Season with salt and pepper and bring to a boil.

Cover and simmer for 30 minutes or until the potatoes are soft. Lift the fish out of the pan with a slotted spoon and transfer to a plate. Discard the bay leaf.

Loosen the bones, if using a Finnan haddock, with a small knife, then lift away the backbone and head. Using a knife and fork break the fish into flakes and lift off the skin. If using haddock fillet, simply peel off the skin and then break the fish into flakes, double-checking there are no bones. Return two-thirds of the fish to the pan then puree the soup in batches in a blender or food processor until smooth. Pour back into the saucepan and stir in the milk and cream. Bring just to a boil, then simmer gently until reheated. Taste and adjust the seasoning if needed.

Ladle into bowls, sprinkle with the remaining fish and the chopped parsley. Serve with toasted barley bannocks or soda griddle scones.

For Scottish ham & haddie bree, add 6 diced bacon slices when frying the potato until it is just beginning to turn golden. Add the fish, bay leaf, stock, and seasoning and simmer gently as above. Lift the fish out of the soup and flake, then return to the soup with the milk and cream and serve as a chunky soup topped with chopped chives.

cajun red bean soup

Serves **6**

Preparation time **25 minutes,
plus overnight soaking**

Cooking time **1 hour**

2 tablespoons **sunflower oil**

1 large **onion**, chopped

1 **red bell pepper**, halved,
cored, and diced

1 **carrot**, diced

1 **baking potato**, diced

2–3 **garlic cloves**, chopped
(optional)

2 teaspoons **mixed Cajun
spice**

13 oz can **chopped tomatoes**

1 tablespoon **brown sugar**

4 cups **vegetable stock** (see
page 13)

14 oz can **red kidney beans**,
drained

⅓ cup sliced **okra**

½ cup thinly sliced **green
beans**

salt and **pepper**

Heat the oil in a large skillet. Add the onion and fry for 5 minutes until softened. Add the red pepper, carrot, potato, and garlic, if using, and fry for 5 minutes. Stir in the mixed Cajun spice, tomatoes, sugar, stock, and plenty of salt and pepper and bring to a boil.

Add the drained beans and mix together. Bring to a boil, then cover and simmer for 45 minutes until the vegetables are tender.

Add the sliced green vegetables, re-cover, and cook for 5 minutes until just cooked. Ladle the soup into bowls and serve with crusty bread.

For Hungarian paprika & red bean soup, make up the soup as above adding 1 teaspoon of paprika instead of the Cajun spice. Simmer for 45 minutes, omit the green vegetables, then puree and reheat. Ladle into bowls and serve topped with 2 tablespoons of sour cream and a few caraway seeds.

seafood & corn chowder

Serves **6**

Preparation time **40 minutes**

Cooking time **35 minutes**

2 tablespoons **butter**

½ bunch of **scallions**,
    trimmed, sliced, white and
    green parts kept separate

2 cups diced **potatoes**

1¼ cups **fish stock** (see
    page 13)

1 large **bay leaf**

5 oz **smoked haddock**

5 oz **haddock** or **cod**

⅓ cup **frozen corn**

7 oz **frozen seafood
    selection**, defrosted, rinsed,
    and drained

1¼ cups **milk**

⅔ cup **heavy cream**

2 tablespoons fresh chopped
    parsley

salt and **pepper**

6 large **bread rolls**, tops
    sliced off and centers
    hollowed out to make a
    bread casing (optional)

Heat the butter in a saucepan, add the white sliced scallions and the potato, toss in the butter then cover and fry gently for 10 minutes, stirring occasionally until only just beginning to brown.

Pour in the stock, add the bay leaf then lay the fish fillets on top and season with salt and pepper. Bring to a boil then cover and simmer gently for 20 minutes until the potatoes are tender. Lift the fish out of the soup with a slotted spoon, put on a plate and peel away the skin. Flake into pieces, carefully checking for any bones.

Return the fish to the saucepan, add the green scallion tops, the frozen corn, defrosted seafood, and milk. Bring back to a boil then cover and simmer for 5 minutes until the seafood is reheated. Discard the bay leaf. Pour in the cream, add the parsley, then taste and adjust the seasoning if needed. Bring back to a boil then ladle into hollowed-out bread rolls. Scoop out the soup with a small spoon then eat the bread last when steeped in all the fishy flavors.

For chicken & corn chowder, add the diced meat of 6 small skinned and boned chicken thighs to the white scallions and fry for 5 minutes until just turning golden. Add 2 cups diced potato then cover and fry gently for 5 minutes. Pour in 1¼ cups chicken stock, add 1 large bay leaf and seasoning. Cover and simmer gently for 30 minutes. Add the green scallion slices, frozen corn, 2 oz diced cooked ham, and the milk. Simmer gently for 5 minutes then mix in the heavy cream. Serve in bread rolls or bowls.

vietnamese beef pho

Serves **6**

Preparation time **15 minutes**

Cooking time **about 45 minutes**

1 teaspoon **sunflower oil**

1 teaspoon **Szechuan peppercorns**, roughly crushed

1 **lemon grass stem**, sliced

1 **cinnamon stick**, broken into pieces

2 **star anise**

1½ inch piece of **fresh ginger root**, peeled, sliced

small bunch of **cilantro**

6 cups **beef stock** (see page 12)

1 tablespoon **fish sauce**

juice of **1 lime**

4 oz **fine rice noodles**

8 oz **sirloin or stir-fry beef steak**, fat trimmed, meat thinly sliced

1 cup **bean sprouts**, rinsed

4 **scallions**, thinly sliced

1 large **mild red chili**, thinly sliced

Heat the oil in a saucepan, add the peppercorns, lemon grass, cinnamon, star anise, and ginger and cook for 1 minute to release their flavors. Cut the stems from the cilantro and add the stems to the pan with the stock. Bring to a boil, stirring, then cover and simmer for 40 minutes.

Strain the stock and return to the pan. Stir in the fish sauce and lime juice. Cook the noodles in a pan of boiling water as directed on the package then drain and divide between 6 small bowls. Add the steak to the soup and cook for 1−2 minutes. Divide the bean sprouts, scallions, and chili between the bowls, then ladle the soup on top and finish with the remaining cilantro leaves, torn into pieces.

For Vietnamese shrimp soup, make up the flavored broth as above, using 6 cups chicken or vegetable stock (see pages 10 and 13) and 2 kaffir lime leaves instead of the cinnamon. Simmer for 40 minutes then drain and finish as above, adding 7 oz raw peeled shrimp and 1½ cups sliced button mushrooms instead of the steak. Cook for 4−5 minutes until the shrimp are pink. Finish with bean sprouts, scallions, and chili as above.

greek chicken avgolomeno

Serves **6**

Preparation time **10 minutes**

Cooking time **15–20 minutes**

8 cups **chicken stock** (see page 10)

4 oz **orzo, macaroni,** or **other small pasta shapes**

2 tablespoons **butter**

¼ cup **all-purpose flour**

4 **egg yolks**

grated zest and juice of 1 **lemon**

salt and **pepper**

To garnish (optional)

4 oz cooked **chicken,** torn into fine shreds

extra **lemon zest**

oregano leaves

lemon wedges

Bring the stock to a boil, add the pasta, and simmer for 8–10 minutes until just tender. Meanwhile, heat the butter in a separate smaller pan, stir in the flour then gradually mix in 2 ladlefuls of the stock from the large pan. Bring to a boil, stirring. Take off the heat.

Mix the egg yolks in a medium-size bowl with the lemon zest and some salt and pepper. Gradually mix in the lemon juice until smooth. Slowly mix in the hot sauce from the small pan, stirring continuously.

Stir a couple more hot ladlefuls of stock into the lemon mixture once the pasta is cooked, then pour this into the large pasta pan. (Don't be tempted to add the eggs and lemon straight into the pasta pan or it may curdle.) Mix well, then ladle into shallow soup bowls and top with shredded chicken taken off the carcass, some extra lemon zest, and some torn oregano leaves. Serve with lemon wedges.

For cod avgolomeno, bring 8 cups strained fish stock to a boil in a large saucepan, add 4 oz small pasta shapes and 1¼ lb skinned cod fillet, simmer for 8–10 minutes until both are tender. Break the fish into flakes, discarding the skin and any bones. Make the sauce with the butter and flour as above then mix in some of the stock, the egg yolks and lemon mix. Add this to the pasta and fish, then ladle into bowls and top with snipped chives or a little snipped chervil.

mushroom hot & sour soup

Serves **4–6**

Preparation time **5–10 minutes**

Cooking time **about 15 minutes**

5 cups **fish stock** (see page 13)

1 **lemon grass stalk**, lightly bruised

3 **dried kaffir lime leaves** or 3 pieces of **lime peel**

2 **Thai red chilies**, halved and seeded

2 tablespoons **lime juice**

1–2 tablespoons **Thai fish sauce**

⅓ cup **canned bamboo shoots**

4 oz **oyster mushrooms**

2 **scallions**, finely sliced

½ **red chili**, sliced, to garnish

Pour the fish stock into a saucepan, add the lemon grass, lime leaves or peel, and chilies. Simmer for 10 minutes. Strain the liquid into a clean saucepan. Reserve a little of the red chili from the sieve and discard the remaining seasonings.

Add the lime juice and fish sauce to taste to the stock with the bamboo shoots, mushrooms, and reserved chili. Simmer for 5 minutes. Ladle the soup into individual bowls and sprinkle with the scallions. Garnish with fresh red chili slices.

For vegetarian tomato hot & sour soup, make the soup following the method above, but use 5 cups of vegetable stock (see page 13) in place of the fish stock, and use 2 tablespoons light soy sauce in place of the fish sauce. Stir in 4 skinned, seeded, and chopped tomatoes and 1½ seeded and diced red bell peppers instead of the mushrooms.

italian tortellini in brodo

Serves **6**

Preparation time **10 minutes**

Cooking time **about 10 minutes**

1 lb **tomatoes**

6 cups **chicken stock** (see page 10)

¾ cup **dry white wine**

1 tablespoon **sundried tomato paste**

small bunch **basil**, roughly torn into pieces

10 oz package **spinach and ricotta tortellini**, or filling of your choice

6 tablespoons freshly grated **Parmesan cheese**, plus extra to serve

salt and **pepper**

Make a cross cut in the base of each tomato, put into a bowl, and cover with boiling water. Allow to soak for 1 minute, then drain and peel away the skins. Quarter the tomatoes, scoop out the seeds, and dice the flesh.

Put the tomatoes into a saucepan, add the stock, wine, and tomato paste, season with salt and pepper, and bring to a boil. Simmer gently for 5 minutes.

Add half the basil and all the pasta, bring back to a boil and cook for 3–4 minutes until the pasta is just cooked. Stir in the Parmesan, taste, and adjust the seasoning if needed. Ladle into bowls, serve with a little extra grated Parmesan, and garnish with the remaining basil leaves.

For gnocchi & pesto broth, flavor 6 cups chicken stock with tomatoes, wine, and sundried tomato paste as above. Add 2 tablespoons pesto and bring to a boil. Add 10 oz chilled gnocchi instead of tortellini and 2½ cups shredded spinach. Simmer for 5 minutes until the gnocchi rise to the surface and the spinach has wilted. Stir in the freshly grated Parmesan and finish as above.

hungarian chorba

Serves **6**
Preparation time **25 minutes**
Cooking time **2½ hours**

1 tablespoon **sunflower oil**
1 lb **stewing lamb on the bone**
1 **onion**, finely chopped
1 **carrot**, roughly chopped
5 oz **rutabaga**, roughly chopped
2 teaspoons **smoked paprika**
¼ cup **long-grain rice**
small bunch **dill weed**, plus extra, torn, to garnish
6 cups **lamb stock** (see page 12)
4–6 tablespoons **red wine vinegar**
2 tablespoons **brown sugar**
2 **eggs**
salt and **pepper**

Heat the oil in a large saucepan, add the lamb and brown on one side, turn over and add the onion, carrot, and rutabaga and cook until both sides of the lamb are browned.

Sprinkle with the paprika, cook briefly, then add the rice, dill, and lamb stock. Spoon in the vinegar, sugar, and plenty of salt and pepper then bring to a boil, stirring. Cover and simmer for 2½ hours until the lamb is very tender.

Lift the lamb out of the saucepan with a slotted spoon, transfer to a cutting board, and cut the meat into small pieces, discarding the bones and fat. Return the lamb to the pan. Beat the eggs in a bowl, gradually mix in a ladleful of hot soup then pour into the saucepan. Heat gently until the soup has thickened slightly, but do not boil or the eggs will scramble. Taste and adjust the seasoning and vinegar if needed. Garnish with extra torn dill and ladle into bowls. Serve with sliced pumpernickel bread.

For chicken & kohlrabi chorba, fry 6 chicken thighs in place of the lamb. Add the onion and carrot and then add 5 oz peeled and diced kohlrabi in place of the rutabaga. Continue as above, simmering for just 1½ hours.

thai shrimp broth

Serves **4**

Preparation time **15 minutes**

Cooking time **about 10 minutes**

5 cups **vegetable stock** (see page 13)

2 teaspoons **ready-made Thai red curry paste**

4 dried **kaffir lime leaves**, torn into pieces

3–4 teaspoons **Thai fish sauce**

2 **scallions**, sliced

5 oz **shiitake mushrooms**, sliced

4 oz **dried soba (Japanese) noodles**

½ **red bell pepper**, cored, seeded, and diced

2 cups **bok choy**, thinly sliced

8 oz **frozen shrimp**, defrosted and rinsed

small bunch of **cilantro leaves**, torn into pieces

Pour the stock into a saucepan, add the curry paste, lime leaves, fish sauce to taste, scallions, and mushrooms. Bring to a boil and simmer for 5 minutes.

Bring a separate pan of water to a boil, add the noodles, and cook for 3 minutes.

Add the remaining ingredients to the soup and cook for 2 minutes until piping hot.

Drain the noodles, rinse with fresh hot water, and spoon into the base of 4 bowls. Ladle the hot shrimp broth over the top and serve immediately with small bowls of Thai fish sauce and dark soy sauce for seasoning, if desired.

For Thai tamarind broth, put the stock into a pan, add 2 teaspoons tamarind concentrate and ¼ teaspoon turmeric, then the curry paste and flavorings as above. Simmer for 5 minutes and continue as above, omitting the shrimp.

chicken soup with lockshen

Serves **6**
Preparation time **20 minutes**
Cooking time **5 minutes**

8 cups **chicken stock** (see
   page 10)
5–7 oz cooked, shredded
   chicken
4 oz **lockshen** (vermicelli
   pasta)
salt and **pepper**
chopped **parsley**, to garnish
   (optional)

Bring the stock to a boil in a large saucepan, add the
shredded chicken, and heat thoroughly. Meanwhile,
bring a second pan of water to a boil, add the lockshen,
and simmer for 4–5 minutes until tender.

Drain the lockshen, divide it between soup bowls, so
that it makes a small nest in the base of each, then
ladle the soup on top. Garnish with a little parsley,
if desired.

For chicken soup with kneidlech, make up the soup
as above, omitting the lockshen. Put ¾ cup medium
matzo meal into a bowl with a pinch of ground ginger,
salt and pepper, and 1 beaten egg. Add 1 tablespoon
melted schmalz (chicken fat available from Kosher
butchers) or nondairy margarine then mix in 5–6
tablespoons of hot chicken stock or water to make a
moldable dough. Divide into 20, shape into small balls,
and chill on a plate for 1 hour. Add to a saucepan of
simmering water and cook for 25 minutes until they
rise to the surface of the water and are spongy. Drain
well and add to bowls of the chicken soup.

ghanaian groundnut soup

Serves **6**

Preparation time **15 minutes**

Cooking time **about 40 minutes**

1 tablespoon **sunflower oil**

1 **onion**, finely chopped

2 **carrots**, diced

1 lb **tomatoes**, skinned if desired, roughly chopped

½ teaspoon **piri piri seasoning** or **dried red pepper flakes**

½ cup **roasted salted peanuts**

4 cups **fish** or **vegetable stock** (see page 13)

To garnish

dried red pepper flakes

peanuts, roughly chopped

Heat the oil in a saucepan, add the onion and carrot, and fry for 5 minutes, stirring until softened and just turning golden around the edges. Stir in the tomatoes and piri piri and cook for 1 minute.

Grind the peanuts in a spice mill or blender until you have a fine powder like ground almonds. Stir into the tomatoes, add the stock and then bring to a boil. Cover and simmer for 30 minutes. Mash or puree half the soup and reheat. Taste and adjust the seasoning if needed, then ladle into bowls, garnish with red pepper flakes and peanuts, and serve with foo foo (see below).

For homemade foo foo, to serve as an accompaniment, peel and cut 1½ lb yam or potatoes into chunks and cook in a saucepan of boiling water for 20 minutes until tender. Drain and mash with 3 tablespoons milk and seasoning. Shape into balls and serve separately for dunking into the hot soup.

chicken mulligatawny

Serves **6**
Preparation time **15 minutes**
Cooking time **about 1¼ hours**

1 tablespoon **sunflower oil**
1 **onion**, finely chopped
1 **carrot**, diced
1 **dessert apple**, peeled,
  cored, and diced
2 **garlic cloves**, finely
  chopped
8 oz **tomatoes**, skinned if
  desired, roughly chopped
4 teaspoons **medium curry
  paste**
⅓ cup **golden raisins**
⅔ cup **red lentils**
6 cups **chicken stock** (see
  page 10)
4 oz **leftover cooked chicken**,
  cut into shreds
salt and **pepper**
cilantro sprigs, to garnish

Heat the oil in a saucepan, add the onion and carrot, and fry for 5 minutes, stirring until softened and just turning golden around the edges. Stir in the apple, garlic, tomatoes, and curry paste and cook for 2 minutes.

Stir in the golden raisins, lentils, and stock. Season with salt and pepper and bring to a boil, cover, and simmer for 1 hour until the lentils are soft. Mash the soup to make a coarse puree. Add the cooked chicken, heat thoroughly then taste and adjust the seasoning if needed. Ladle into bowls and garnish with cilantro sprigs. Serve with warm naan bread or pappadams.

For citrus carrot mulligatawny, fry the onion with 1 lb diced carrots in 2 tablespoons sunflower oil for 5 minutes. Omit the next five ingredients, then add the red lentils, the grated zest and juice of 1 orange and ½ lemon, and 6 cups vegetable stock (see page 13). Bring to a boil, cover, and simmer for 1 hour. Puree until smooth then reheat and adjust seasoning. Serve with croutons (see page 15).

london particular

Serves **6**

Preparation time **25 minutes** plus soaking time

Cooking time **1 hour 20 minutes**

1 ½ cups **dried green split peas**, soaked overnight in cold water

2 tablespoons **butter**

4 **bacon slices**, diced

1 **onion**, roughly chopped

1 **carrot**, diced

2 **celery sticks**, diced

6 cups **ham** or **chicken stock** (see pages 10 and 11)

salt and **pepper**

To garnish

handful of **parsley**, chopped

4 **bacon slices**, broiled and snipped

Drain the peas into a colander. Heat the butter in a large saucepan, add the bacon and onion, and fry for 5 minutes until softened. Add the carrot and celery and fry for 5 more minutes, stirring until golden.

Add the peas and stock and bring to a boil, stirring. Boil rapidly for 10 minutes then reduce the heat, cover, and simmer for about 1 hour or until the peas are tender.

Allow the soup to cool slightly then puree half the soup in batches in a blender or food processor until smooth. Return to the saucepan and reheat. Add salt and pepper to taste.

Ladle the soup into bowls then sprinkle the parsley and bacon over the top.

For mixed pea broth, soak 1 ½ cups soup mix (a blend of yellow and green split peas, pearl barley, and red lentils) in cold water overnight. Make up the soup as above adding this instead of the soaked green split peas. Serve topped with 4 slices bread cut from a white bread roll, toasted, then spread with 2 tablespoons butter mixed with 2 teaspoons anchovy relish or 3 finely chopped and drained canned anchovies.

tomato & bread soup

Serves **4**
Preparation time **10 minutes**
Cooking time **35 minutes**

2 lb **really ripe vine
tomatoes**, skinned, seeded,
and chopped
1¼ cups **vegetable stock**
(see page 13)
6 tablespoons **extra virgin
olive oil**
2 **garlic cloves**, crushed
1 teaspoon **sugar**
2 tablespoons chopped **basil**
4 oz **ciabatta bread**
1 tablespoon **balsamic
vinegar**
salt and **pepper**
basil leaves, to garnish

Place the tomatoes in a saucepan with the stock,
2 tablespoons of the oil, the garlic, sugar, and basil and
gradually bring to a boil. Cover the pan and simmer
gently for 30 minutes.

Crumble the bread into the soup and stir over a low
heat until it has thickened. Stir in the vinegar and the
remaining oil and season with salt and pepper to
taste. Serve immediately or allow to cool to room
temperature, if preferred. Garnish with basil leaves.

For tomato & bread soup with roasted peppers,
halve 1 red and 1 orange bell pepper, scoop out the
seeds then put cut side downward in a broiler pan,
brush with 1 tablespoon of olive oil then broil for
10 minutes until the skins have charred. Wrap in foil
and cool. Peel off the skins and slice. Add to a
saucepan with 3 lb skinned and seeded tomatoes and
the stock, oil, garlic, sugar, and basil as above. Bring
to a boil then continue as above.

caribbean pepper pot soup

Serves **6**

Preparation time **20 minutes**

Cooking time **about 50 minutes**

2 tablespoons **olive oil**

1 **onion**, finely chopped

1 **Scotch bonnet chili**, seeded, finely chopped or 2 **hot Thai red chilies**, chopped with seeds

2 **red bell peppers**, cored, seeded, and diced

2 **garlic cloves**, finely chopped

1 large **carrot**, diced

2 cups diced **potatoes**

1 **bay leaf**

1 **thyme sprig**

1¾ cups **full-fat coconut milk**

2½ cups **beef stock** (see page 12)

salt and **cayenne pepper**

To garnish

7 oz **sirloin steak**

2 teaspoons **olive oil**

Heat the oil in a saucepan, add the onion, and fry gently for 5 minutes until softened and just beginning to turn golden. Stir in the chili, red pepper, garlic, carrot, potato, and herbs and fry for 5 minutes, stirring.

Pour in the coconut milk and beef stock, then season with salt and cayenne pepper. Bring to a boil, stirring, then cover and simmer for 30 minutes or until the vegetables are tender. Discard the herbs, then taste and adjust the seasoning if needed.

Rub the steak with the oil then season lightly with salt and cayenne pepper. Heat a griddle or skillet and when hot add the steak and fry for 2–5 minutes on each side to taste. Allow to stand for 5 minutes then slice thinly. Ladle the soup into bowls, garnish with the steak slices, and serve with crusty bread.

For shrimp & spinach pepper pot soup, make up the soup as above using 2½ cups fish stock (see page 13) in place of the beef stock. Simmer for 30 minutes, then add 7 oz raw peeled shrimp, defrosted if frozen, and 2½ cups spinach. Cook for 3–4 minutes until the shrimp are pink and cooked through and the spinach is just wilted.

french onion soup

Serves **4**
Preparation time **15 minutes**
Cooking time **1 hour**

2 tablespoons **butter**
2 tablespoons **olive oil**
1 lb large **onions**, halved and
   thinly sliced
1 tablespoon **superfine sugar**
3 tablespoons **brandy**
⅔ cup **red wine**
4 cups **beef stock** (see
   page 12)
1 **bay leaf**
salt and **pepper**

Cheesy croutes
4–8 slices **French bread**
1 **garlic clove**, halved
1½ oz **Gruyère cheese**,
   grated

Heat the butter and oil in a saucepan, add the onions and toss in the butter, then fry very gently for 20 minutes, stirring occasionally, until very soft and just beginning to turn golden around the edges.

Stir in the sugar and fry the onions for 20 minutes more, stirring more frequently toward the end of cooking until the onions are caramelized to a rich dark brown. Add the brandy and, when bubbling, flame with a long taper and quickly stand well back.

Add the wine, stock, bay leaf, salt, and pepper as soon as the flames subside, then bring to a boil. Cover and simmer for 20 minutes. Taste and adjust the seasoning if needed.

Toast the bread on both sides then rub with the cut surface of the garlic. Sprinkle with the cheese and put back under the broiler until the cheese is bubbling. Ladle the soup into bowls and top with the cheesy croutes.

For apple & onion soup, fry the onions as above and add 1 small peeled, cored, and grated cooking apple along with the sugar. When the onions are caramelized, flame with 3 tablespoons Calvados or brandy then add ⅔ cup hard cider, 4 cups chicken stock, and 2 fresh thyme sprigs. Simmer for 20 minutes. Serve with garlic toasts topped with sliced broiled Camembert and sprinkled with a little extra thyme.

russian borshch

Serves **6**
Preparation time **15 minutes**
Cooking time **55 minutes**

2 tablespoons **butter**
1 tablespoon **sunflower oil**
1 **onion**, finely chopped
12 oz uncooked **beet**,
  trimmed, peeled, and diced
2 **carrots**, diced
2 **celery sticks**, diced
1 ¼ cups chopped **red
  cabbage**
2 ½ cups diced **potato**
2 **garlic cloves**, finely
  chopped
6 cups **beef stock** (see
  page 12)
1 tablespoon **tomato paste**
6 tablespoons **red wine
  vinegar**
1 tablespoon **brown sugar**
2 **bay leaves**
salt and **pepper**
¾ cup **sour cream**
small bunch of **dill weed**

Heat the butter and oil in a saucepan, add the onion, and fry for 5 minutes until softened. Add the beet, carrot, celery, red cabbage, potatoes, and garlic and fry for 5 minutes, stirring frequently.

Stir in the stock, tomato paste, vinegar, and sugar. Add the bay leaves and season well with salt and pepper. Bring to a boil then cover and simmer for 45 minutes until the vegetables are tender. Discard the bay leaves then taste and adjust the seasoning if needed.

Ladle into bowls and top with spoonfuls of sour cream, torn dill fronds, and a little black pepper. Serve with rye bread.

For vegetarian borshch with pinched dumplings, soak 1 cup dried mushrooms in 1 ¼ cups boiling water for 15 minutes. Make up the soup as above, omitting the beef stock, adding the soaked mushrooms and their liquid plus 5 cups vegetable stock (see page 13) instead. For the dumplings, mix 1 cup white flour, ¼ teaspoon caraway seeds, salt and pepper, 2 beaten eggs, and enough water to mix to a smooth dough. Shape into a sausage, pinch off pieces, and add to the soup, simmering for 10 minutes until spongy. Omit the cream and dill.

fragrant tofu & noodle soup

Serves **2**
Preparation time **15 minutes,
   plus 10 minutes draining**
Cooking time **10 minutes**

4 oz firm **tofu**, diced
1 tablespoon **sesame oil**
3 oz thin **dried rice noodles**
2½ cups **vegetable stock**
   (see page 13)
1 inch piece of **fresh ginger
   root**, peeled and thickly
   sliced
1 large **garlic clove**, thickly
   sliced
3 **dried kaffir lime leaves**,
   torn in half
2 **lemon grass stalks**, halved,
   lightly bruised
handful of **spinach** or **bok
   choy leaves**
½ cup **bean sprouts**, rinsed
1–2 fresh **red chilies**, seeded
   and finely sliced
2 tablespoons **cilantro leaves**
1 tablespoon **Thai fish sauce**
lime wedges, to serve

Put the tofu on a plate lined with paper towels and allow to stand for 10 minutes to drain.

Heat the oil in a wok until hot and fry the tofu for 2–3 minutes until golden brown, stirring frequently.

Meanwhile, soak the noodles in boiling water for 2 minutes, then drain.

Pour the stock into a large saucepan. Add the ginger, garlic, lime leaves, and lemon grass and bring to a boil. Reduce the heat, add the tofu, noodles, spinach or bok choy, bean sprouts, and chilies and heat through. Add the cilantro and fish sauce, then pour into deep bowls. Serve with lime wedges and chili sauce.

For tofu & satay soup, fry the tofu as above. Add the ginger and garlic to the stock, omitting the lime leaves and lemon grass. Stir in 2 tablespoons crunchy peanut butter and 1 tablespoon soy sauce. Simmer for 3 minutes, then add the tofu, noodles, spinach or bok choy, bean sprouts, and chilies. Serve with cilantro and lime wedges.

corn & chicken chowder

Serves **4–6**
Preparation time **15 minutes**
Cooking time **about 30 minutes**

2 tablespoons **butter** or **margarine**
1 large **onion**, chopped
1 small **red bell pepper**, cored, seeded, and diced
1 ¼ lb **potatoes**, diced
¼ cup **all-purpose flour**
3 cups **chicken stock** (see page 10)
¾ cup **canned** or **frozen corn**
8 oz **cooked chicken**, chopped
1 ¾ cups **milk**
3 tablespoons chopped **parsley**
salt and **pepper**
few **red chilies**, sliced, to garnish

Melt the butter or margarine in a large saucepan. Add the onion, red pepper, and potatoes and fry over a moderate heat for 5 minutes, stirring from time to time.

Sprinkle in the flour and cook over a gentle heat for 1 minute. Gradually stir in the stock and bring to a boil, stirring. Lower the heat, cover the pan, and cook for 10 minutes.

Stir in the corn, chicken and milk. Season to taste with salt and pepper, cover the pan, and simmer gently for 10 minutes more, until the potatoes are just tender. Taste and adjust the seasoning if necessary. Serve the chowder garnished with the sliced chilies and parsley.

For ham & corn chowder, fry the onion, bell pepper, and potato in the butter as above. Add the flour then stir in the stock and simmer for 10 minutes. Meanwhile broil an 8 oz smoked ham steak for 10 minutes, turning once, then trim off the fat and dice the ham. Stir into the soup with the corn, milk, and parsley and finish as above.

basque fish soup

Serves **6**

Preparation time **20 minutes**

Cooking time **45 minutes**

2 tablespoons **olive oil**

1 **onion**, finely chopped

½ **green bell pepper**, cored,
seeded, and diced

½ **red bell pepper**, cored,
seeded, and diced

1 **zucchini**, diced

2 **garlic cloves**, finely
chopped

8 oz **potatoes**, cut into chunks

½ teaspoon **smoked paprika**

⅔ cup **red wine**

4 cups **fish stock** (see
page 13)

13 oz can **chopped tomatoes**

1 tablespoon **tomato paste**

2 **whole mackerel**, gutted,
rinsed with cold water inside
and out

salt and **cayenne pepper**

Heat the oil in a large saucepan, add the onion, and fry gently for 5 minutes until softened. Add the peppers, zucchini, garlic, and potato and fry for 5 minutes, stirring. Mix in the paprika and cook for 1 minute.

Pour in the red wine, fish stock, tomatoes, tomato paste, salt, and cayenne pepper. Bring to a boil, stirring, then add the whole mackerel. Cover and simmer gently for 20 minutes until the fish flakes easily when pressed with a knife.

Lift the fish out with a slotted spoon and put on a plate. Simmer the soup uncovered for an additional 15 minutes. Peel the skin off the fish then lift the flesh away from the backbone. Flake into pieces, checking carefully for any bones.

Return the mackerel flakes to the pan. Reheat and ladle into shallow bowls. Serve with lemon wedges and crusty bread.

For Portuguese fish soup, make up the soup as above, omitting the smoked paprika and adding 2 bay leaves. Simmer for 20 minutes without the fish then add 1 lb of mixed tuna, cod, or hake steaks and 8 oz scrubbed closed mussels instead of the mackerel. Cook for 10 minutes or until the mussels have opened then lift out both the mussels and the fish steaks. Flake the fish into pieces, discarding the skin. Remove the mussel shells and discard any closed mussels. Return the fish and mussels to the pan and serve sprinkled with chopped cilantro.

index

236

acknowledgments

Executive Editor Nicky Hill
Editor Kerenza Swift
Executive Art Editor Mark Stevens
Designer Peter Gerrish
Photographer William Shaw
Home Economist Sara Lewis
Props Stylist Liz Hippisley
Production Assistant Vera Janke

Commissioned Photography © Octopus Publishing Group Ltd/William Shaw apart from the following:
© **Octopus Publishing Group Limited**/Diana Miller 67, 117; Gareth Sambridge 167, 177; Ian Wallace 139; Lis Parsons 179; Sandra Lane 175, 185; Sean Myers 33; Simon Smith 25, 29, 47, 87, 105, 181, 207; Stephen Conroy 16, 79, 101, 121, 163, 193, 199; William Lingwood 39, 51, 191, 213, 231; William Reavell 21, 45, 95, 171, 187, 189, 233.